JOURNAL OF ROMANIAN STUDIES

Vol. 1, No. 1 (2019)

JRS editors
Lavinia Stan and **Margaret Beissinger**

JRS review editor
Radu Cinpoes

About the Society for Romanian Studies

THE SOCIETY FOR ROMANIAN STUDIES (SRS) *is an international interdisciplinary academic organization, founded in 1973, that is dedicated to promoting the professional study, criticism, and research of all aspects of Romanian culture and society, particularly concerning the countries of Romania and Moldova. The SRS is generally recognized as the major professional organization for North American scholars concerned with Romania, Moldova, and their diasporas.*

SRS is affiliated with the South East European Studies Association (SEESA); the Association for Slavic, East European and Eurasian Studies (ASEEES—formerly known as the American Association for the Advancement of Slavic Studies or AAASS); the American Political Science Association (APSA); the American Historical Association (AHA); and the Romanian Studies Association of America (RSAA).

SRS offers a number of programs and activities to its members, including the peer-reviewed *Journal of Romanian Studies*, a biannual newsletter, the Romanian Studies book series published in collaboration with the publishing house Polirom in Iași, a mentoring program, prizes for exceptional scholarship in two different categories, as well as an international conference organized every three years in Romania.

More information about the SRS, including current officers, the national board, and membership information, can be found on the SRS website at *https://society4romanianstudies.org*.

www.society4romanianstudies.org
The Society for Romanian Studies

Editorial Board:

LAVINIA STAN (lstan@stfx.ca) and
MARGARET BEISSINGER (mhbeissi@Princeton.EDU)
JRS editors

RADU CINPOES (Radu.Cinpoes@kingston.ac.uk)
JRS review editor

Advisory Board:

DENNIS DELETANT (Georgetown University, USA)

JON FOX (University of Bristol, UK)

VALENTINA GLAJAR (Texas State University, USA)

PETER GROSS (University of Tennessee, USA)

BRIGID HAINES (Swansea University, UK)

IRINA LIVEZEANU (University of Pittsburgh, USA)

MIHAELA MIROIU (National School of Political Science
and Public Administration, Romania)

STEVE D. ROPER (Florida Atlantic University, USA)

DOMNICA RADULESCU (Washington and Lee University, USA)

PAUL E. SUM (University of North Dakota, USA)

CRISTIAN TILEAGA (Loughborough University, UK)

VLADIMIR TISMANEANU (University of Maryland, College Park, USA)

LUCIAN TURCESCU (Concordia University, Montreal, Canada)

Bibliographic information published by the Deutsche Nationalbibliothek
The Deutsche Nationalbibliothek lists this publication in the Deutsche Nationalbibliografie; detailed bibliographic data are available on the Internet at http://dnb.dnb.de.

Bibliografische Information der Deutschen Nationalbibliothek
Die Deutsche Nationalbibliothek verzeichnet diese Publikation in der Deutschen Nationalbibliografie; detaillierte bibliografische Daten sind im Internet über http://dnb.d-nb.de abrufbar.

Journal of Romanian Studies
Vol. 1, No. 1 (2019)

Stuttgart: *ibidem*-Verlag / *ibidem* Press

Erscheinungsweise: halbjährlich / Frequency: biannual

ISBN 978-3-8382-1294-4

ISSN 2627-5325

Ordering Information:
PRINT: Subscription (two copies per year): € 58.00 / year (+ S&H: € 4.00 / year within Germany, € 7.00 / year international). The subscription can be canceled at any time.
Single copy or back issue: € 34.00 / copy (+ S&H: € 2.00 within Germany, € 3.50 international).

E-BOOK: Subscription (two copies per year): € 35.99 / year, individual copy or back issue: € 24.99 / copy. Available via ibidem.eu.
For further information please visit www.ibidem.eu

© *ibidem*-Verlag / *ibidem* Press
Stuttgart, Germany 2019

Alle Rechte vorbehalten
Das Werk einschließlich aller seiner Teile ist urheberrechtlich geschützt. Jede Verwertung außerhalb der engen Grenzen des Urheberrechtsgesetzes ist ohne Zustimmung des Verlages unzulässig und strafbar. Dies gilt insbesondere für Vervielfältigungen, Übersetzungen, Mikroverfilmungen und elektronische Speicherformen sowie die Einspeicherung und Verarbeitung in elektronischen Systemen.

All rights reserved

No part of this publication may be reproduced, stored in or introduced into a retrieval system, or transmitted, in any form, or by any means (electronical, mechanical, photocopying, recording or otherwise) without the prior written permission of the publisher.
Any person who performs any unauthorized act in relation to this publication may be liable to criminal prosecution and civil claims for damages.

Printed in the EU

Contents

Editorial Note
LAVINIA STAN, MARGARET BEISSINGER AND RADU CINPOES 7

A Subjective Centenary: The Peasant Footprint in Recent Romanian History
VINTILĂ MIHĂILESCU 9

Notes on a Century of Surveillance
KATHERINE VERDERY 35

Shattered Illusions: Britain and Iuliu Maniu, 1940–1945
DENNIS DELETANT 53

The Queen Is No Sister: Three Faces of Marie of Romania
MARIA BUCUR 77

Stalinism and Anti-Stalinism in Romania: The Case of Alexandru Jar Revisited
MARIUS STAN AND VLADIMIR TISMANEANU 105

Katherine Verdery, My Life as a Spy: Investigations in a Secret Police File.
Review by RADU CINPOES 123

Cristian Vasile ed., "Ne trebuie oameni!": Elite intelectuale și transformări istorice în România modern și contemporană.
Review by ROLAND CLARK 127

Ioana Em. Petrescu & Liviu Petrescu, Scrisori Americane (1981-1983), Ediție îngrijită, studiu introductiv, notă asupra ediției și note de Ioana Bot, postfață de Liana Vescan.
Review by IULIU RAȚIU 131

Bruce O'Neill, The Space of Boredom. Homelessness in the Slowing Global Order.
Review by PETRU NEGURA 135

Editorial note

With the support of ibidem press, we are happy to launch the *Journal of Romanian Studies* (JRS) on behalf of the Society for Romanian Studies, which this year celebrates 45 years since its inception in 1973. The *JRS* is meant to strengthen Romanian Studies as a field by gathering high quality manuscripts dealing with all aspects of Romanian culture and society, particularly concerning the countries of Romania and Moldova, as well as the Romanian diaspora living in other countries. As *JRS* editors, we are committed to upholding the integrity of the peer-review process and helping authors to improve their contributions. We envision the publication of two issues per year, each including five to eight research articles and up to four book reviews.

The first issue opens with the two keynote speeches delivered by Profs. Vintila Mihailescu and Katherine Verdery at the international conference the SRS organized in June 2018 in Bucharest. These anthropologists explore the significance of two well-known topics – peasants and intelligence services – at the centenary of the Romanian modern state. Dennis Deletant uses previously unavailable archives to trace the British perception of Iuliu Maniu in 1940-1945, and the steps taken by the British Foreign Office and the British Special Operations Executive to encourage him to bring about the overthrow of Marshall Ion Antonescu. In her article, Maria Bucur provides a gender analysis of Queen Marie of Romania as a politician/diplomat, participant in the military campaign, and supporter of feminists' effort to gain the vote during World War I. Marius Stan and Vladimir Tismaneanu, by contrast, focus on the lesser known Romanian communist Alexandru Jar as the most prominent Romanian case of disenchantment with Stalinism. These research articles are followed by three book reviews.

We would like to thank Jakob Horstmann for his unflinching support of the *JRS*, and Valerie Lange for her outstanding help with nailing down the details of the *JRS* and putting this issue together.

JRS Advisory Board: Dennis Deletant (Georgetown University, USA), Jon Fox (University of Bristol, UK), Valentina Glajar (Texas State University, USA), Peter Gross (University of Tennessee, USA), Brigid Haines (Swansea University, UK), Irina Livezeanu (University of Pittsburgh, USA), Mihaela Miroiu (National School of Political Science and Public Administration, Romania), Steve D. Roper (Florida Atlantic University, USA), Domnica Radulescu (Washington and Lee University, USA), Paul E. Sum (University of North Dakota, USA), Cristian Tileaga (Loughborough University, UK), Vladimir Tismaneanu (University of Maryland, College Park, USA), Lucian Turcescu (Concordia University, Montreal, Canada).

Lavinia Stan (lstan@stfx.ca) and **Margaret Beissinger** (mhbeissi@Princeton.EDU)
JRS editors

Radu Cinpoes (Radu.Cinpoes@kingston.ac.uk)
JRS review editor

A Subjective Centenary: The Peasant Footprint in Recent Romanian History

The peasants do not speak, they are spoken about. (Pierre Bourdieu)

Vintilă Mihăilescu

Abstract: *This article approaches Romanian history from the perspective of the peasantry. It treats the role of the peasantry throughout the modern period as well as some of the legacies it has transmitted up to the present day. The history of Romania's peasantry is viewed in the Balkan context. Beyond various similarities and differences between the neighbouring countries, significant is the fact that the large agrarian properties lasted much longer in Romania than in the rest of the Balkans. This explains why the last great peasant revolt in the history of Europe took place in Romania (1907) and why Romania is still the largest agrarian, rural country in Europe, with a land distribution identical to that in 1905. The article also identifies what present-day Romanian society has inherited from this long-lasting peasant culture and its structural peculiarities, focusing on the broad, all-encompassing consequences of its enduring "orality" (i.e., lack of "graphic reason"). This article was originally delivered as the first keynote address on 26 June 2018 at the triennial Society for Romanian Studies conference held in Bucharest.*

A centenary invites reflection. My present reflection on the centenary of Greater Romania (1918–2018) is elective and biased because it discusses the country's modern history by focusing on the role of the peasantry and its legacies to date. In doing so, I have in mind not only the fact that the "peasant question" (*chestiunea țărănească*) is a defining continuity of the Romanian *longue durée*, but also that its premises and consequences in time and space are frequently underestimated and/or embedded in canonic narratives of the *Romanian Being*.

Premises and Context of the "Peasant Question." The Past of the Present

The Great Union almost doubled the population of the Old Kingdom, which in 1918 represented 48.72 percent of the total population of Greater Romania. The rural population of the new state represented 81 percent of the total population. The Old Kingdom had a smaller rural population (76.4 percent) than Transylvania and Banat (82.7 percent), while Bukovina had even less (73.4 percent) and Bessarabia much more (87.2 percent). These regions had different historical backgrounds and different socio-cultural and economic specificities inherited from the three empires they had depended on previously: the Ottoman, the Habsburg and the Russian Empires. Here I refer only to the "Balkan context" because I consider it representative for the socio-economic context of all of the peasantry living in the Romanian territories in *general*, despite its diversity.

The Balkan Context

Traian Stoianovich may be correct when considering that nothing "fundamentally" new happened in the Balkans from the Neolithic age until the early 19th century.[1] This *stagnation* may largely explain why as early as 1500 a major economic gap divided the Balkans from the West, and why "the sweeping structural changes that turn growth into development would not appear in the Balkans until after the Second World War."[2] Such "stagnation" means neither a lack of social change, nor a "development-resistant culture," as Lawrence Harrison and Samuel Huntington labelled it.[3] Daniel Chirot wrote that "Eastern Europe's failure to keep up was not so unusual as to need a special explanation. Eastern Europe, or most of it, was more like the rest of the world, slow to change and progress."[4] I will therefore distinguish *stagnation* (i.e., being "slow to change") from *growth* and *development* (in the modern capitalist sense).

The Balkans started to be "backward" only after the West (in fact, some parts of it) advanced ahead of the rest of the world. "Economic gaps" became relevant only when "economic development" became the

---

[1] Pavel Moraru, *La hotarul românesc al Europei: Din istoria Siguranței generale în Basarabia, 1918–1940* (Bucharest: Institutul Național pentru Studiul Totalitarismului, 2008), 24.

[2] John R. Lampe, "Imperial Borderlands or Capitalist Periphery? Redefining Balkan Backwardness, 1520–1914," in *The Origins of Backwardness in Eastern Europe. Economics and Politics from the Middle Ages Until the Early Twentieth Century*, ed. by Daniel Chirot (Berkeley, CA: University of California Press, 1989), 202.

[3] Lawrence E. Harrison and Samuel P. Huntington, *Culture Matters: How Values Shape Human Progress* (New York: Basic Books, 2000).

[4] Daniel Chirot, *The Origins of Backwardness in Eastern Europe. Economics and Politics from the Middle Ages until the Early Twentieth Century* (Berkeley, CA: University of California Press, 1989), 4.

point of reference in a global economy where the Balkans were on the "periphery." Like other states on the periphery of the global economy such as Brazil or Portugal, Romania started its capitalist history from the position of "classic dependency," as noticed by Peter Evans, by relying mainly on primary exports (agricultural products, ores, hydrocarbons).[5] This kind of development is much too volatile and exposed to the pressure of competitors to ensure a rapid development. This situation can be overcome by "semi-periphery dependency," a socioeconomic purgatory where the jump into industrialization takes place, usually at the initiative of state elites. This "jump" came late in Romania – only in the 1930s.[6]

Some of the causes of these waves of stagnation-cum-growth were directly or indirectly linked to the peasantry and they should be reminded here. For a long time, *the population density in the Balkans* was not very different from the rest of Europe, but in the Balkans it remained very low much longer. According to Michael Palairet, the average population density in the Ottoman Balkans was 12.9 inhabitants per square kilometre in 1800, and 35.7 in 1900. Belgium, in contrast, had 128 inhabitants per square kilometre as early as 1831.[7] It was only in the late 19th century that the Balkan states reached, and occasionally exceeded, the threshold of 30–40 inhabitants per square kilometre. In Romania, the population density increased from 33 inhabitants per square kilometre in 1859, to 45.3 in 1899 and 50 in 1906, thus surpassing the European average of 41.6. The "density of Balkan settlement in the early 19th century was too low to permit an efficient division of labour in utilizing the natural endowment."[8] This indicator is essential if we consider that "overcoming this threshold meant a crossroad of economic development (...) Land became a relatively scarce resource and the demographic pressure compelled people to reduce the land used for raising cattle in favour of land allocated to agriculture" and to introduce more productive agricultural exploitation methods.[9]

---

5   Peter Evans, *Dependent Development: The Alliance of Multinational, State and Local Capital in Brazil* (Princeton: Princeton University Press, 1979), quoted in Cornel Ban, *Dependență și dezvoltare. Economia politică a capitalismului românesc* (Bucharest: Editura Tact, 2014).
6   Ban, *Dependență și dezvoltare*, 15.
7   Michael Palairet, *The Balkan Economies c. 1800–1914. Evolution without Development* (Cambridge: Cambridge University Press, 1997).
8   Ibid., 22.
9   Bogdan Murgescu, *România și Europa. Acumularea decalajelor economice (1500–2010)* (Iași: Polirom, 2010), 100.

Table 1. Degree of Urbanization as Percentage of People Living in Localities with More than 5,000 and 2,000 Persons

	1800		1850		1910	
	5000 crit.	2000 crit.	5000 crit.	2000 crit.	5000 crit.	2000 crit.
Europe	10.9%	15.0%	16,4%	20.3	32.9%	36.2%
Romania	7.5%	11.8%	11.0%	15.2%	16.0%	20.0%
Bulgaria	5.5%	9.8%	6.0%	10.3%	22.1.0%	25.9%
Greece	11.5%	15.5%	14.0%	18.0%	21.0%	25.8%
Serbia	10.0%	14.2%	10.0%	14.2%	9.8%	14.2%

Source: Paul Bairoch and Gary Goertz, "Factors of Urbanisation in the Nineteenth Century Developed Countries: A Descriptive and Econometric Analysis," *Urban Studies*, 23 (1986): 285–305.

The *rural/urban ratio*. The Balkans lacked strong cities connected by large commercial networks – with the exception of Istanbul, and later on of a few other local centres, such as Thessaloniki and Bucharest. Following the criteria of a town having more than 2,000 or 5,000 inhabitants, during the 19th century Greece alone was more urbanized than the average European state, but had a lower density at the beginning of the 20th century (see Table 1). If we use the urbanization index, which considered a town to be a locality with more than 10,000 inhabitants, Europe had 360 towns in 1800 and 878 in 1850, yielding an urban population of 10 and 16.7 percent, respectively. In contrast, in Eastern Europe (Austria-Bohemia and Poland) only 4.2 percent of the population lived in urban areas in 1800, and 7.5 percent in 1850.[10] The percentage was lower in the Balkans. Intensive urbanisation came to the region only by the mid-19th century, and affected mainly the capital cities.

The rural population of the Balkans was not much larger than in most of Europe, but it remained so for a much longer period of time. At the end of World War II, Albania, Bulgaria, Yugoslavia and Romania were 75 to 80 percent rural; Greece was only 63 percent. Romania remains one of the most rural countries in Europe (see Table 2).

Agriculture and property relations. Stoianovich's continuing stagnation may best apply to agriculture, where substantial improvements were late to come. Productivity in agriculture very slowly improved by the end of 19th century. In 1938, it represented only 52 percent of the European average in Bulgaria and 38 percent in Romania.[11] Around 1930, over 90 percent of all farms in the Balkans had up to 10 hectares, compared to just 20 percent in Germany or 8 percent in the United

---

10   Jan de Vries, *European* Urbanization *1500–1800* (London: Routledge, 1984).
11   Measured as dollar per person working in agriculture. Murgescu, *România și Europa*, 241.

Kingdom.¹² The young Balkan nation-states have tried to change this land distribution and achieve social justice mainly by reducing the land and power of the great landowners. Thus,

> at the beginning of the 20th century, with the exception of Romania, big properties were virtually inexistent. In Bulgaria, landowners with more than 100 hectares represented 0.1 percent of all landowners and had 3.8 percent of the agricultural land, while in Serbia this category covered only 0.3 percent of all landowners and had only 0.1 percent of the rural land. Big properties remained only in Romania, as the 1864 land reform gave landowners more than half of the land they had previously owned.¹³

Table 2.   The Rural Population as Percentage of Total Population (1989 and 2017)

	1989	2017
EU	29.65%	24.74%
Albania	63.84%	40.68%
Bulgaria	33.97%	25.42%
Greece	28.72%	21,35%
Hungary	34.19%	27.89%
Moldavia	53.51%	54.79%
Romania	47.49%	45.05%
Poland	38.77%	39.45%
Serbia (1990)	49.60%	44.20%
Ukraine	33,28%	29.86%

Source: World Bank, *Rural population (% of total population)*, 2018, available at: https://data.worldbank.org/indicator/SP.RUR.TOTL.ZS, accessed on 11 October 2018.

In 1921 the number and land plots of large landowners were significantly reduced. This and the numerous very small household plots of land (see Table 7) reduced land productivity. In fact, the Romanian land reforms have remained *agrarian* (focused on property) more than *agricultural* (focused on productivity) in nature.¹⁴ I agree with Bogdan Murgescu that at the beginning of the 20th century "the contrast between the 5,000 landlords owning more than half of the land and the 85 percent of the peasants having less than five hectares each is the key to agrarian

---

12   David Turnock, *Eastern Europe: An Historical Geography 1815–1945* (London: Routledge, 1990), 90.
13   Ștefan Dorondel and Stelu Șerban, "A Missing Link: The Agrarian Question in Southeast Europe," *Martor*, 19 (2014): 14.
14   Constantin Garoflid, "Regimul agrar în România," in *Enciclopedia României* (Bucharest: Imprimeria Națională, 1939), vol. 1, 557–585, and Béatrice von Hirschhausen, *Les nouvelles campagnes roumaines. Paradoxes d'un 'retour' paysan* (Paris: Belin, 1997).

relations in the Romanian Principalities (*Vechiul Regat*)."[15] Improvements in agriculture were generally a precondition for industrial development, but not in the Balkans where a poorly developed agriculture, which employed more than 80 percent of the active population, delayed industrial development.

Table 3.   GDP per Capita (1870–2017)

	1870	1890	1913	1929	1937	1950	1989	1950/ 1989	2017
Albania						1.001	2.477	147%	4.582
Bulgaria	809	1.087	1.450	1.128	1.496	1.651	6.216	276%	7.351
Greece	986	1.009	1.454	2.135	2.509	1.915	10.111	428%	18.637
Romania	1.143	1.395	1.705	1.102	1.206	1.176	3.460	194%	10.757
Serbia/ Yugoslavia	599	843	1.060	1.364	1.273	1,546	5.470	354%	5.899
Total Europe	1.686		2.677	2.882	3.217				
Western Europe						5.005	17.579	251%	
EU									41.174

Sources: Stephen Broadberry and Alexander Klein, *Continental, Regional and National Data with Changing Boundaries* (2011), 19, 24 and 28, available at: https://www.nuffield.ox.ac.uk/users/Broadberry/Euro GDP2 (accessed 15 August 2018); Angus Maddison, *The World Economy. A Millennial Perspective* (Paris: OECD, 2010); and International Monetary Fund, *World Economic Outlook Database*, April 2018, available at: https://www.imf.org/external/pubs/ft/weo/2018/01/weodata/weoselco.aspx?g=%2020 01&sg=All+countries, accessed on 11 October 2018.

By considering *overall economic development* as reflected by GDP per capita levels, we can sketch the main trends of development in the Balkans and the rest of Europe (see Tables 3 and 4). According to Maddison, "in the year 1000, Asia (except Japan) produced more than two thirds of the world GDP, Western Europe less than 9 percent. In 1820, the proportions were 56 and 24 percent, respectively. In 1998, the Asia share was about 30 percent compared with 46 percent for Western Europe and Western offshoots combined." Thus, Western Europe and Western offshoots had a faster rate of growth: "in 1000–1820, their average per capita income grew nearly four times as fast as the average for the rest of the world. The differential continued between 1820 and 1998 when per capita income of the first group rose 19-fold and 5.4-fold for the second. (…) By 1820, [these countries] had forged ahead to a level about

---

15   Murgescu, *România și Europa*, 100.

twice that of the rest of the world. In 1998 the gap was almost 7:1."[16] In comparison, Eastern Europe started its economic growth from a lower base (667 GDP per capita compared with 1,232 in Western Europe in 1820) and improved its performance at a much slower rate. Its growth in GDP per capita was 550 percent between 1820 and 1998, compared with 1,350 percent for Western Europe, and its annual average growth rate was 1.06 compared with 1.51. The Balkan countries started their capitalist development as part of the global periphery, and faced a growing economic gap with the West despite their unequal but considerable growth. The geopolitical position of "periphery" placed the whole region in the category of "dependent development" from the beginning.

The unequal economic development started in the 19th century all over the Balkans was ambivalent. Given the region's backwardness, the growth is impressive, but compared with the European average is, as Palairet called it, an "evolution without development."[17] It remains the source of both pride and shame in the region.

Table 4.   GDP per Capita as Percentage of the European Average (100%)

Country	1870	1913	1937	1950	1990	2007*	2016*
Albania				28%	23%	23%	29%
Bulgaria	48%	54%	46%	34%	51%	40%	49%
Yugoslavia/Serbia	36%	40%	40%	43%	52%	33%	37%
Romania	68%	64%	37%	33%	33%	43%	58%
Greece	58%	54%	78%	50%	94%	93%	68%

* GDP/capita in PPP$
Source: Stephen Broadberry and Alexander Klein, *Continental, Regional and National Data with Changing Boundaries*, 2011, available at:
https://www.nuffield.ox.ac.uk/users/Broadberry
/Euro GDP2, accessed on 15 August 2018; and Eurostat, *GDP per Capita, Consumption per Capita and Price Level Indexes*, 2017 https://ec.europa.eu/eurostat/statisticsexplained/index.php/GDP_per_capita,_consumption_per_capita_and_price_level_indices#Relative_volumes_of_GDP_per_capita, accessed on 11 October 2018.

Romania had a relatively good start in the late 19th century, as its GDP per capita and share of the European average were the highest in 1870. But the gap between Romania and the EU has increased: on the eve of its EU accession in 2007, Romania's GDP per capita was 2.5 times lower than the European average (in 1870 it was only 1.5 times lower). These statistics challenge two complementary master narratives in Romania:

---

16   Angus Maddison, *The World Economy. A Millennial Perspective* (Paris: OECD, 2010), 27.
17   Palairet, *The Balkan Economies c. 1800–1914*.

the celebration of the interwar period and the demonization of the communist one.

In 1937, Romania's GDP per capita was lower than in 1913 and its share of European average decreased to 37 percent (see Table 4). The 1929 world crisis had disastrous consequences, as Greater Romania's strategies for economic development were inadequate, and its social development was far below European, even regional, levels.[18] After World War I, Romania's economic growth took off, without reaching Western levels. Industrial production grew by 80 percent in 1925–1938 and the share of industrial workers in the total population doubled, without surpassing 7 percent.[19] In 1937, Romania ranked second in Eastern Europe after Yugoslavia in terms of industrialization, but its industrialization represented only 5.9 percent of Great Britain's and its industrial productivity remained the lowest in Europe.[20] The 1921 land reform reduced social inequalities, but also productivity and export levels. In 1938, Romania's agricultural productivity was one of the lowest in Europe ($80/person), smaller than Bulgaria's.[21] Thus, "at the end of the inter-war period Romania had not really started the restructuring of its agricultural production."[22] Moreover, the purchasing power of the rural population decreased, thus limiting the effect of industrialization: "the domestic market demand was disabled by the poverty of the villages."[23]

I doubt that without the communist "break" Romania would have become a "normal developed country,"[24] as Romanians believe. In terms of its GDP per capita, Romania lost ground during the interwar period and caught up during communism. Communism did not hijack Romania's "natural" journey to modernization. On the contrary, despite the dramatic and unquestionable socio-political and human costs registered in 1945–1989, modernization indicators such as industrialization, urbanization and social development (literacy, health care, housing, etc.)

---

18 In the 1930s, life expectancy at birth was 40.29 for men and 41.40 for women, child mortality was 197; health care was provided by 1.1 doctors for 10.000 inhabitants, and alimentation in calories was 2760/day. Murgescu, *România și Europa*.
19 Turnock, quoted in Ban, *Dependență și dezvoltare*, 34.
20 Murgescu, *România și Europa*.
21 Laurențiu Ivanov, *A Study of the Inter-war Economies of Poland and Romania*, paper presented at The 7th International Days of Statistics and Economics, Prague, 19–21 September 2013, available at: https://msed.vse.cz/files/2013/123-Laurentiu-Ivanov-paper.pdf, accessed on 15 August 2018.
22 Ibid., 772.
23 Murgescu, *România și Europa*, 266.
24 Ban, *Dependență și dezvoltare*, 40.

had exceptional growth rates under communism,[25] but the inner contradictions of the communist development model made them unsustainable in the long run. Nevertheless, by 1989 the GDP per capita gap between Romania and Europe was double that of 1870, and at the time of Romania's EU accession in 2007 the share of its GDP per capita as percentage of the European average barely reached 43. Even in the new millennium, Romania remained an underdeveloped, highly rural and agrarian European country.[26] In 2017, Romania still had the largest share of the population working in agriculture (23.7 percent, compared to the EU average of 4.5) and the smallest number of full-time workers in agriculture (1.5 percent, compared with the EU average of 16.4). By all means, the "peasant/agricultural question" is still unsolved...

Table 5. Rural Development and Agriculture in Romania around Year 2000

	Gross Value Added as % of GDP 2002	Workforce in agriculture as % of the total population 2002	Organic area as % of the total surface, 2000	Share of food expenses in household's total budget, 2002
EU 15	1.6%	4.3%	40.6%	16.2 %
CEEC 10	4.6%*	13.4%	54.4%*	28.3%
Estonia	2.9%	6.5%	22.1%	32.7%
Hungary	3.1%	6.1%	62.9%	27.7%
Latvia	2.9%	15.3%	38.5%	32.9%
Lithuania	2.1%	18.6%	53.4%	38.9%
Poland	2.5%	19.6%	58.3%	28.0%
Slovakia	2.1%	6.6%	49.8%	28.7%
Czech Republic	1.2%	4.9%	54.3%	26.4%
Slovenia	2.1%	9.7%	24.2%	22.0%
Bulgaria	9.7%	10.7%	50.3%	31.8%
Romania	13.4%	36.4%	62.1%	39.9%

Source: Dumitru Sandu, *Dezvoltarea rurală și reforma agricuturii românești* (Bucharest: Centrul Român pentru Politici Economice, 2004).

---

25   In 1989, the volume of industrial production was 44 times greater than in 1950, and 65 times greater than in 1938. Murgescu, *România și Europa*, 341; David Turnock, *Aspects of Independent Romania's Economic History with Particular Reference to Transition for EU Accession* (Aldershot: Ashgate, 2007).

26   Violette Rey, Octavian Groza, Ioan Ianoș and Maria Pătroescu, *Atlas de la Roumanie* (Paris: CNRS-Libergéo et La Documentation française, Paris, 2000).

Social Organisation and the Culture of Peasant Society in Romania

The Romanian peasant communities had a different history than in Western Europe. In the West,

> it was from the beginning a question of a landowning class and their warrior enemies who, by conquest, assumed the social status of landowners, and of a serf class which gradually liberated itself. In the east, the peasants, organized into free village communities, fell into serfdom quite late, to the benefit of nobles either only recently risen from local "chieftainships" or evolved from conquerors of areas which they had colonized in western fashion. The feudal lords of the east exploited not only slaves or conquered peoples but also free village communities by purely fiscal means, and only much later acquired property rights over the land and the inhabitants.[27]

The "communal village" (*obște devălmașă*) was the matrix of social organization of peasant collectives in Moldavia and Walachia. It was only when the communal village lost ground and communal possessions turned into genealogical ownership that the "archaic *obște*" transformed into "*sate umblătoare pe moși*" (villages treading on ancestors) and the economic lineage of the *neam* (descent group) asserted itself in the life of the *obște*. Only then did kinship replace residence.

What is particular to this social organization? For Emanuel Todd, Romania's "nuclear egalitarian family"[28] was characterized by "liberty and equality" similar to northern France, Italy, central Portugal, Greece and Poland. A more accurate description should consider the family/household not in itself, but embedded in its relations with the surrounding village community. Here, Max Weber's distinction between "domestic community" and "neighbourhood" (*Nachbarschaft*) may prove inspiring. The former refers to "a community which covers the needs for work and relationships," "a domestic communism with no deliberate distribution, as each member brings his own contribution according to his capabilities, while meeting his necessary needs (provided there are

---

27 Henri H. Stahl, *Traditional Romanian Village Communities: The Transition from the Communal to the Capitalist Mode of Production in the Danube Region* (London and Paris: Cambridge University Press and Editions de la Maison des Sciences de l'Homme, 1979), 7.

28 For Todd, the nuclear category involved the non-cohabitation of maried sons with their parents. In egalitarian nuclear families, the equality of heritage between offsprings is the rule; absolute nuclear families have no such rule. Emanuel Todd, *La Troisième Planète. Structures familiales et systèmes idéologiques* (Paris: Seuil, 1983).

enough available goods)."²⁹ The latter term refers to "extraordinary" needs, and it "does not define only the 'primitive' form of relations occurring as a result of field proximity or of people inhabiting those places, but also, in general, it defines the entire community of interests, be they ephemeral or perennial, which result from the geographical proximity or the residential space of more or less permanent residents."³⁰ Weber assigns to these neighbourhoods the characteristics of economic "brotherhood" or "fraternity" of the "mutual help offered in the absence of any sentimentality.³¹

The *obște*-like social organisation may be better understood in comparison with the neighboring South-Slav *zadruga*, which is a communal family in Todd's understanding, an "extended family," or the *Hauskommunion* provided by the Habsburg code of laws.³² A *zadružna kuća* household inhabited by an "extended" or "multiple" family can include over 50 people. Thus, "domestic communism" is large enough to cover most "necessary needs" so that the "economic brotherhood" of the *Nachbarschaft* loses importance.

In contrast, the Romanian households are nuclear families of parents and unmarried children, with only the last child expected to cohabit with the parents until their death. In Romania "the village as a whole was communal, not the extended family,"³³ and "village responsibilities [were] emphasized far more than kin responsibilities."³⁴ The communal villages were territorial, not family based, units. Consequently, Romanian families were considerably smaller than the zadrugas.³⁵ Romanian villages are larger, but have smaller individual households. Stoianovich confirmed the inverse ratio between the "domestic community" and the

---

29 Max Weber, *Economie et société* (Paris: Plon, 1971), 379 and 83–84.
30 Ibid., 380.
31 Ibid., 382.
32 For Todd, a communal family implies the equality of heritage between offsprings and the cohabitation with parents after marriage. Zadruga is "a household made of two or more biological or small families, closely related through blood or adoption and having in common the means of production, while producing and consuming their means of joint life and regulating together the control of property, work and means of life." Philip E. Mosley, *Essays by Philip E. Mosely and Essays in His Honor* (Notre Dame: University of Notre Dame Press, 1976), 19; and Karl Kaser, "Die Entwicklung der Zadruga in der kroatisch-slawonischen Militärgrenze," *Zur Kunde Südosteuropas*, II/14 (1985), 14–25.
33 Chirot, "The Romanian Communal Village," 141.
34 Margaret Mead, "Introduction: Philip E. Mosely's Contribution to the Comparative Study of the Family," in *Communal Families in the Balkans: The Zadruga. Essays by Philip E. Mosely and Essays in His Honor*, ed. by Robert F. Burnes (Notre Dame: University of Notre Dame Press, 1976), xxiv.
35 Chirot, "The Romanian Communal Village," 153.

"neighbourhood" when he claimed that during the 18th century in Serbia the regions with the smallest villages had the largest households, while towards the east, where agriculture (not herding) prevailed, extended families were very rare.[36] In Romania, the social organisation of peasant communities focused on the "neighborhood" of the *obște devălmașă* more than the "household" (*gospodărie*).

A two-fold consequence is important here. First, "the smallest social unit" of the village started by being the village itself and ended by being "households, not individuals."[37] Even today, Adam Drazin notes, "the Romanian idea of domesticity presumes the collectivity of the household and not the welfare or care for its individual members."[38] Second, the "spirit of the *obște*" (*duhul devălmaș*[39]) lasted longer than the *obște* and informed land reforms up to the eve of Greater Romania. In 1906, Vasile Kogălniceanu complained that "twenty-five years have passed since the rural law has been implemented, and the land of those appropriated in 1864 is still not delimited. In each village, the rulers divided the land into two parts: the part for the landlord and the part for the locals, without delimiting the land due to each villager, so that locals still possess their land in severalty [shared land]."[40] In 1918, the land reform stipulated that "the appropriated land must be cultivated in the *obște*."[41] In this social organisation of the peasant communities village solidarities were stronger and lasted longer, being only partially replaced by kin, and later on by household solidarities. This was hardly propitious for the emergence of modern individualism...

The *obști devălmașe* and *sate umblătoare pe moși* were described by Henri Stahl, but the Saxon-rooted *Nachbarschaft* (*vecinătate/vecinie*) is less known to Romanians,[42] although it spread over a large part of Transylvania, in towns and villages alike, under the Habsburg administration. (The main exception were the pastoral communities of

---

36 Stoianovich, *Balkan Worlds.*
37 Paul H. Stahl, "L'organisation magique du territoire villageois roumain," *L'homme*, 13, 3 (1973), 150.
38 Adam Drazin, "A Man Will Get Furnished: Wood and Domesticity in Urban Romania," in *Home Possessions. Material Culture behind Closed Doors*, ed. by Daniel Miller (Oxford: Berg, 2001), 196.
39 Henri Stahl, "Organizarea socială a țărănimii," *Enciclopedia României* (Bucharest: Imprimeria Națională, 1938), vol. I, 559–577.
40 Vasile Kogălniceanu, *Chestiunea* țărănească (Bucharest: Joseph Göbl, 1906), 18.
41 Garoflid, "Regimul agrar în România," 581.
42 Henri Stahl, "Vecinătățile din Drăguș," *Sociologie Românească*, 1, 1(1936), 18–31; Candid Mușlea, "Contribuții la instituția Veciniei la românii brașoveni," *Studii și articole de istorie*, II (1957), 317–344; and Vintilă Mihăilescu, ed., *Vecini și Vecinătăți în Transilvania* (Bucharest: Paideia, 2003).

Mărginimea Sibiului.) The *Nachbarschaft* is based on territory and includes some 40–50 households on a street. It is not an *a priori* status, as membership in a clan (*neam*) or ethnic group: theoretically, one has to gain entry and may lose membership status. The *Nachbarschaft* is ruled by an elected "Father," not a soft gerontocracy as the *obști*, and all its activities are stipulated by a written Statute, violations of these written norms being fined according to their gravity (*Bussgeld*). This "moral book-keeping" makes the difference: *de facto*, what peasants were supposed to do in their communities is about the same for both the *obste* and the *Nachbarschaft*, but *Nachbarschaft* members had obligations as part of a written contract, while for the *obște* member it was a matter of shame and pride controlled only by "*gura satului*" (the oral judgement of the village). The difference between Transylvania's organisation in *Nachbarschaften* and the rest of Romania's organisation in *obști* should be kept in mind when speaking about "the Romanian peasant."

Table 6. Ungureni and Pământeni

		Ungureni	Pământeni
Biological differences	Kretschmer types	Pyknic	Leptosomic
	Blood pressure	Higher	Lower
	Reactivity to effort	hypo-reactivity	hyper-reactivity
	Reaction time	reflectivity: low speed & fewer omissions	impulsivity: high speed & more omissions
Psychological differences	Cognitive styles	field independence	field dependence
		external locus of control	internal locus of control
		lower conformism	higher conformism
	Intelligence	abstract intelligence	concrete intelligence
	Moral styles	autonomy	heteronomy
	Linguistic styles	socio-centric	ego-centric
		Abstract	Concrete
		more nouns	more verbs
Cultural differences	Ritual performing	group performed & formalized	more individually performed & diverse

An important difference divides *shepherds and farmers*. I did fieldwork for almost twenty years in northern Oltenia, in communities of *ungureni* (sheep-raisings) and *pământeni* (mainly farmers) with low rates of intermarriages until World War II. Two constellations of distinctive traits could be observed, suggesting that there were at least two "Romanian peasants with different (sub)cultures. From the iconic pastoral ballad Miorița to the folklorist Ovid Densușianu ("we are a pastoral people," he claimed in 1914) or the philosopher Constantin Noica (speaking about "our pastoral soul" in 1944), it is the shepherd who is perceived as the "true" Romanian peasant.[43]

Peasants into Romanians

In *Peasants into Frenchmen*, Eugen Weber explained "how undeveloped France was integrated into the modern world and the official culture – of Paris, of the cities."[44] Romania's nation-building process was similar, but Romania had no Paris! "While towns were becoming more alike," wrote Weber, "country people continued to show a remarkable diversity from one region to another and even from one province to the next."[45] Before becoming a nation, Romania was a "country of counties" and local identity was highly prevailing, as in the rest of the Balkans. Around 1870, half of the French population was composed of farmers and peasants, whom the Parisians perceived as the 'other' and 'imagined' as "vulgar, hardly civilized, their nature meek but wild."[46] At that time, Romania's population was 85 percent rural, and even if the social distance between the local boyars and the peasants was much smaller than in France and there was almost no ethnic Romanian bourgeoisie, the perception of the peasant as "the other" and the "inner primitive" was just as marked as in France.[47]

How to turn peasants into Frenchmen or Romanians? Weber suggests that the nation had to be constructed by the state (or Paris), spurred on by some exogenous shock (in France, industrialization), or developed through a combination of the two. However, Romanian's industrialization was slow and delayed. Romanians had no state strong enough to build national consciousness, so that they had to rely on the

---

43 An experimental research on intelligence concluded that peasants in mountain and hilly regions, mostly shephards, are more intelligent than those from the plains, mainly farmers. Constantin Rădulescu-Motru and I.-M. Nestor, *Cercetări experimentale asupra inteligenței la români* (Bucharest: Monitorul Oficial și Imprimeria Statului Imprimeria Națională, 1948).
44 Eugen Weber, *Peasants into Frenchmen: The Modernization of Rural France 1870–1914* (Stanford: Stanford University Press, 1976), 6.
45 Ibid., 9.
46 Ibid., 4.
47 Alecu Russo pretended that local boyars and free peasants are the same old Volk. See Ovidiu Bîrlea, *Metoda de cercetare a folclorului* (Bucharest: Editura pentru literatură, 1974).

idea of a previously existing "nation." Mihai Eminescu claimed that "peoples are not a product of intelligence, but of nature,"[48] while for Nae Ionescu "what prevails is the nation; the state is, in a way, only its means."[49] This "proto-nation"[50] existing from *illo tempore* had to become the subject of nation-building. In all Balkan agro-pastoral societies, the political solution to the nation-building task was to recast the invisible peasant–the only available Volk–into the stakeholder of the emerging "nation," the "people" who had inhabited this territory since time immemorial. There was a problem: this proto-nation, the people, the presumed Volk, was not aware of his status and historic mission. Turning peasants into Romanians was difficult. Ionescu-Gion complained that "only some years ago, if asking a peasant: 'What about you, my friend, what are you?', he was answering, pretty embarrassed: 'Eh, Sir, what can I be? I'm a Christian, like everyone else.'"[51] In 1895, a school inspector was shocked to find that "there still are – and they are very many – Romanians who don't know their nationality [*neam*]."[52] As such, the "exogenous shock" that fuelled national awareness in Romania were the independence wars, starting with 1877 and culminating with the "Great War." Before explaining who Romanians are, the question was: *against whom are we Romanians?* The school and the press then melted the Romanian counties into one single country.

Let me mention two long-lasting consequences. First, collective independence overcame individual freedom. In 1858, Simion Bărnuțiu wrote that "the true liberty of any nation can only be national."[53] In turn, Nicolae Bălcescu suggested that "nationality has to be raised above liberty. As long as people do not exist as a nation, it has nothing to do with liberty."[54] Sorin Adam Matei concluded that for Romanians, it was more important to be "independent as a nation, and only (...) in a secondary way free as individual beings. (...) The liberty of the nation is undermin-

---

48 Ioan Stanomir and Laurențiu Vlad, *A fi conservator* (Bucharest: Universitatea din București and Editura Meridiane, 2002), 153.
49 Nae Ionescu, "Stat și nație," 1928, available at: http://anonimus.ro/2014/08/stat-si-natiune-de-nae-ionescu-1928/, accessed on 15 August 2018.
50 Eric Hobsbawm, *Nations and* Nationalism *since 1780: Programme, Myth, Reality* (Cambridge: Cambridge University Press, 1992).
51 Luminița Murgescu, *Între 'bunul creștin' și 'bravul român': rolul școlii primare în construirea identității naționale românești (1831–1878)* (Iasi: Editura A '92, 1999).
52 Ibid.
53 Alex Drace-Francis, *Geneza culturii române moderne. Instituțiile scrisului și dezvoltarea identității naționale 1700–1900* (Iasi: Polirom, 2016).
54 Cited in Sorin Adam Matei, *Boierii minții. Intelectualii români între grupurile de prestigiu și piața liberă a ideilor* (Bucharest: Compania, 2004), 67.

ing the liberty of the individual."⁵⁵ Romanians are still more sensitive to threats to (collective) sovereignty than to attacks on (individual) freedom.

Second, the Romanian peasants were seduced and valued as the icon of the Romanian identity, but abandoned as the boorish others. Culturally patrimonialized, peasants were also socio-economically marginalized. Despite relative economic development, social underdevelopment was significant even during the interwar period. "An expression of social and politic elitism, the social development of the country was purely disastrous."⁵⁶ Urban-rural gaps mounted in post-communism rather than diminishing. Michael Herzfeld notes that,

> for international political and economic audiences, national leaders portray them [the marginal peasant communities] as atypical of the new, modern reality embedded in a complex nexus of global communications. For the often humiliatingly self-abasing tourist trade, and in the romantic folklore of the urban elite, they embody the national quintessence. This disjuncture creates a perennial embarrassment: how is tradition to be recast as modernity, and rebelliousness as a love of (national) independence? For, as the state appropriates for its own purposes the local idioms of morality, custom, and the solidarity of kinship, it dismisses the local renditions themselves as conservative survivals, picturesque tradition, and familism, respectively – all serious obstacles to the European nation-state's rationalist vision of modernity.⁵⁷

Consequences and Heritages. The Present of the Past

Here "heritage" refers to a set of habitual practices that are reproduced over a long period of time with small changes in time and space. In this sense, "heritage" is the very opposite of "tradition." In fact, traditions are an invention of modernity. Tradition is rooted in a selective and elective past that it had abandoned: "tradition is an inverted filiation," as Jean Pouillon wrote, while heritage is a contextual historical filiation.⁵⁸

Several "heritages" are of interest here. First, orality versus "graphic reason." The heritage of the peasant "oral society" is all-embracing but also neglected. Orality is directly linked to illiteracy; given its highly rural population, Romania was also highly illiterate.⁵⁹ In

---

55 Ibid., 67.
56 Ban, *Dependență și dezvoltare*, 35.
57 Michael Herzfeld, *Cultural Intimacy. Social Poetics in the Nation-State* (London: Routledge, 1997), 7.
58 Jean Pouillon, "Tradition: transmission ou reconstruction," *Fétiches sans fétichisme* (Paris: Maspero, 1975), 155–173.
59 The literacy rate in the Principalities was 22 percent in 1899; 15 percent in the rural areas. The rate reached 39.3 percent in 1912, and 57 percent in Greater

a "residual" form, orality may exist in literate societies too. Consequently, the fact that peasant societies in Romania were oral societies is not to be reduced to illiteracy but understood as a lack of "graphic reason."[60] Defining orality as a general cultural praxis of interpersonal communication and social relationships has usually been overlooked by researchers. As Jack Goody noted, "much of the discussion and much of our thinking about other cultures has been based on the misinterpretation of the nature of oral 'tradition'...This is especially true of the politico-legal domain, for the growth of bureaucracy clearly depends to a considerable degree upon the ability to control 'secondary group' relationships by means of written communications."[61] Goody reminds us that for Max Weber "one of the characteristics of bureaucratic organizations was the conduct of official business on the basis of written documents."[62] In short, oral cultures in the Balkans frame time and space, cultural transmission, as well as social and political relations in different ways than in societies based on writing. Even with growing literacy, Romania was missing a "graphic reason" and remained a highly "residual orality" society. This mainly peasant heritage of orality implies six conditions: prevailing oral communication characterizing interpersonal relations, with the consequent downgrading of institutional relations; interpersonal over institutional trust, and thus a "low trust society," insofar as we are speaking of trust in institutions; commitment to interpersonal oral agreements rather than abstract and written norms and contracts; dysfunctional bureaucracy (a bureaucracy is functional when the replacement of any of its members affects none of its clients); a rather fluid temporality and difficulties in strict time management on middle and long term: the master word in this respect is "we'll see" (*mai vedem...*); and *folk lore* knowledge: a relative prevalence of opinion over fact.

Second are *kinship relations*. The household, as discussed earlier, remained the smallest social unit of shared production and consumption for a long time. Its preeminent role consolidated the role of the family–

Romania in 1930 (but only 31 percent in rural areas). In contrast, Hungary reached 85 percent in 1920 and Bulgaria 60.3 percent in 1926. Romania's rate was even lower if we consider that elementary education was unavailable to one-third of the population. Drace-Francis, *Geneza culturii române moderne*, 54; Sabin Manuilă and Mitu Georgescu, "Populația României," *Enciclopedia României*, (Bucharest: Imprimeria Națională, 1938), vol. 1, 133–160.

60 Jack Goody, *The Domestication of the Savage Mind* (Cambridge: Cambridge University Press, 1977), 37.
61 Ibid., 15.
62 Ibid., 27.

and kinship–in making ends meet by flexible strategies of domestic economy. As Rhoda Halperin has pointed out,

> The goal of the family economy is not to ascend the ladder of social stratification; rather, it is to make ends meet by keeping the kin network intact through daily, ongoing economic activities, often in seasonal cycles. (...) Here, occupation is secondary in defining who people are. The family network (who are 'my people') defines self and person. (...) Thus, a family imperative guides people's economic activities. Kinship orders livelihood processes through the pattern of householding.[63]

Although ideologically it opposed peasants and their domestic economy and displaced millions of rural people to towns, the Romanian communist regime did not totally destroy the rural household and its way of life. Industrialization and urbanization transformed the household when some of its members continued to stay in the village while others worked or even lived in cities. These members were bound together by exchanges of goods, services and caring across more or less distant rural-urban networks: the spatial unit of the household was largely replaced by a "diffuse household."[64] During the 1980s economic shortage, these kinship networks of exchanges became an almost unavoidable means for making ends meet. Paradoxically, communism thus reinforced the "traditional family" and its efficient kin networks of helping and caring. This led to the ruralization of cities more than the urbanization of the village, as the communists insisted. Neither did communism attain the "proletarization" of the peasants, since the "New Man" was the "peasant-worker" whom Ivan Szelenyi described in Hungary.

In this long-lasting and renewed household structure, the family, not the individual, was the main social actor. The individual liberation project typical of the modern capitalist life is subordinated to the family project. Even the recent migration strategies have been initially family-based, not individual. This may explain the generational clash between "familist" parents and "individualist" children in the emerging middle-class. Social conflict has been politicised, the "familist" parents being accused of communist nostalgia and electoral misbehaviour, while the young generation embraces progress and modern cosmopolitanism.

Third, *property relations* are embedded in the social relations of peasant communities. They started as communal and non-genealogical, then were divided along genealogical kin-based filiations (*spițe de ne-*

---

63 Rhoda H. Halperin, *Cultural Economics. Past and Present* (Austin: University of Texas Press, 1994), 164.
64 Vintilă Mihăilescu, "La maisnie diffuse, du communisme au capitalisme : questions et hypotheses," *Balkanologie*, 4, 2 (2000), 73–90.

am), and ended up as household land ownerships. All these forms have coexisted, and "the juridical notion of property (...) is replaced by a fact: sharing work in the community."[65] These property relations underpinned the work and exchanges networks of the diffuse households during communism. During post-communism, "sharing work in the community" is again the main strategy to make ends meet in subsistence households.

Some of the old possessions of the *obști* (and also *composesorate, obști de cumpărare, păduri grănicerești, păduri urbariale, comune politice, cooperative*) have been reinvented after 1989 on the basis of old communal documents, but in hesitant juridical terms. When asked about the constitutionality of these arrangements, the Constitutional Court explained that if it were not about "a traditional form of organisation that proved its viability throughout history," the present legal regulations "could have raised constitutional doubts."[66] As such, individual property, in its modern sense, came late into Romanian legal culture.[67] This diversity of property entitlements and their still unclear administrative evidence impede the shift to contractual property, especially when it comes to cadastral evidence in EU terms.

In the countryside, however, property relations had remained embedded in power relations between landlords and peasants. Today, the distribution of land is almost the same as in 1905. "Romania [still] has two agricultures, without any relations between them and with divergent objectives, interests and even development solutions."[68]

---

65 Henri H. Stahl, *Contribuții la studiul satelor devălmașe românești* (Bucharest: Editura Academiei R.P.R., 1959), vol. 2, 123.
66 Virginia Duminică, "Lost in Translation. Despre natura juridică a obștii de moșneni," *Revista Română de Drept Privat*, 6 (2017), 75–110.
67 Katherine Verdery, *The Vanishing Hectare: Property and Value in Postsocialist Transylvania* (Ithaca: Cornell University Press, 2003); and Duminica, "Lost in Translation."
68 CRPE, "O țară și două agriculturi. România și reforma Politicii Agricole Comune a UE," *Policy Memo* 4 (2009), 18.

Table 7.   Land distribution

Year	< 5 ha		5 – 50 ha		> 50 – 100 ha		> 100 ha	
	% farms	% land	% farms	% land	% farms	% land	% farms	% land
1905	77%	26%	22,4%*		25%		0.6%	49%
1920	95.7%	43.8%	3.6%		15.9%		0.7%	40.3%
1930	92%**	73.7%	7.6%***		15.9%		0.4%	10.4%
2005	93.8%	35.5%	5.9%	15.7%	0.3%****		48.8%	
2010	92.8%	29.8%	6.6%	17.5%	0.6%****		52,8%	
2016	91,6%	28.7%	7.8%	20%	0.18%	3.3%	0.37%	47.8%

*) 5–10 ha
**) Less than 10 ha.
***) 10–100 ha
****) More than 50 ha
Sources: Institutul Național de Statistică, *Anuarul Statistic al României 1939 și 1940* (Bucharest: Imprimeria Națională, 1940); Oana Eleonora Glogoveţan, *Evoluția exploataţiilor agricole din România – element fundamental al economiei rurale*, PhD doctoral defense defended at Babeș-Bolyai University, Cluj-Napoca, 2014; and Păun Ion Otiman, "Structura agrară actuală a României – O mare (și nerezolvată) problemă socială și economică a țării," *Revista Română de Sociologie*, 23, 5–6 (2012), 339–360; INS, RGA (2010); INS, ASA (2016)

While the land reforms of 1921 partly addressed this polarization, the post-communist land reforms—focused on property, not productivity, and lacking a clear agricultural strategy—deepened the gap between the "two agricultures."[69] The percentage of farms with less than 1 ha increased from 63 in 2005 to 71 in 2012, but decreased to 53 in 2016. Farms with more than 100 ha represented 0.37 percent in 2016. Hence, the subsistence economy reappeared. In-between, at the beginning of the 20th century, farms with 10 to 50 ha represented 3.7 percent of all farms and owned 8.9 percent of agricultural land; at the time of this writing they represent 1,65 percent and possess 4,5 percent of the land. The politics of property liberalisation and allotment proved inconsistent with the peasants' socio-economic situation and traditional agrarian practices and could not turn peasants into farmers.[70] The failure to inte-

---

69   von Hirschhausen, *Les nouvelles campagnes roumaines*.
70   Dorondel and Șerban, "A Missing Link"; and Cornel Micu, *From Peasants to Farmers? Agrarian Reforms and Modernization in Twentieth Century Romania. A Case*

grate the countryside in the capitalist market is a shortcoming of Romanian capitalism.

Fourth, *juridical relations* have been largely based on oral agreements: for a long time, the *adălmaş* or *aldămaş* (a drink shared by two parties at the end of a successful transaction) was the most common form of sale "contract." In the 19th century (even earlier in Transylvania), juridical agreements were settled "*pe obraz*" (honour-based), and were sometimes doubled by written acts.[71] Years ago, an old peasant with whom I talked refused to legally authenticate his land deed because his grandfather had an *adălmaş* with the former owner – and this was considered sufficient.[72]

Public relations were governed by customary laws ranging from the "right of the land" (*legea ţării*), whose origin and spatial distribution are still debated by legal experts, to the noblemen's "right of the sword" (*dreptul de paloş*), observed until the mid-19th century, and the ubiquitous moral institution of "*gura satului*," so different from the Transylvanian written statute of *vecinătăţi*. Dimitrie Cantemir characterized Romanian juridical relations as *ius non scriptum*.[73] What we inherited from these long-standing customary juridical relations is the fact that we still try to interpret written legal acts and norms using face-to-face agreements, "as between humans" (*ca între oameni*), and that we still have a poor contractual culture.

Equally important is *religion*. Romanians are overwhelmingly Orthodox; even Greco-Catholicism may be considered a political variant of Orthodoxy. Added to this is widespread *orthopraxy*—the particular, local and parochial ways of practicing Christianity. This was made possible by the more flexible (and tolerant) principle of *oikonomia*, allowing

---

Study: Bordei Verde Commune in the Brăila County (Frankfurt am Main: Peter Lang, 2012).

71 Costaforu illustrates an "intermediary type between code and custom" in the interwar period: "in Toader Popa's household, the former generations did not use [written] acts. Everything Toader Popa owns was transferred to him '*pe obraz*,' without acts, not even a dowry leaf. But all the juridical facts he has done himself are accompanied by probative letters. 'I did *zapise* (written proof) for everything (...)' – Popa confesses. Elements of the former customary law have not entirely disappeared [in Popa's household]." Xenia Costaforu, *Cercetarea monographică a familiei. Contribuţie metodologică* (Bucharest: Tritonic, 1945/2004), 322.

72 Vintilă Mihăilescu and Virginia Duminică, "Householding, Tourism, and Market in a Post-Socialist Romanian Village," in *Utopia and Neoliberalism. Ethnographies of Rural Spaces*, ed. by Hana Horakova, Andrea Boskoboinik and Robin Smith (Berlin: Lit Verlag, 2018), 187–211.

73 Dimitrie Cantemir, *Descrierea stării de odinioară şi de astăzi a Moldovei* (Bucharest: Institutul Cultural Român, 1716/2006-2007).

more space in the interpretation and application of the canons, and the Orthodox understanding of *theosis* as the purpose of human life, rooted in a more personal and "mystical" relation to God (different from the Catholic scholastic, "rational" way). The Orthodox Churches permitted diverse local ceremonial practices of "popular religion" to travel across the region. Few laymen understood the cannons (even priests were illiterate, that is, "oral"[74]), but most of them knew how to worship a saint or perform a ritual, and all of them upheld the "true faith." As a "popular religion," Orthodoxy in Romania integrated pre-Christian practices through local orthopraxy; it was "borderline magic," similar to Mircea Eliade's "cosmic Christianity"[75] and opposed to the "ecclesiastic" one. Orthodoxy is not truly a "religion of the Book"; rather worship is a personal activity, and belief in God does not imply trust in the Church and/or the priests.

Religious practices may be confusing for modern, secularist or just more rationalist oriented minds. With 95 percent of Romanians declaring their belief in God in 2018, Romania is one of the most religious countries in Europe. However, only 21 percent of Romanians attend church weekly. In 2013, 61 percent (70 percent in rural areas) of Romanians pray at home, 93 percent of them maintain Sundays and religious holy days and 40 percent fast during Lent. The religious imaginary is "elective": 95 percent of Romanians believe in God, but only 66 percent in life after death; 76 percent believe in Paradise, but only 61 percent in Hell and 54 percent in the Devil. Some 41 percent of Bucharest residents believe in the Evil Eye.[76]

Beyond original "Byzantinism," orthopraxy is interpreted by both Western laic societies and Romanian civic activists as a popular penchant for mysticism typical of "oriental" and "backward" Orthodoxy. The denigration of orthopraxy is another reason to keep it at a distance, as a dark and anti-modern religion that challenges modern European secular traditions. This mass belief may be turned into mass political capital – and this is what happens again today.

We need another Max Weber to describe the Orthodox *work ethic*. A peasant work ethic was theorized by several economists, including

---

74 Drace-Francis, *Geneza culturii române moderne*.
75 Mircea Eliade, *De la Zalmoxis la Ginghis-han* (Bucharest: Editura Științifică și Enciclopedică, 1980).
76 IRES, "Romania credincioasa. Perceptii privind religia si morala," no date, available at: http://www.ires.com.ro/articol/238/august-2013---romania-credincioasa--perceptii-privind-religia-si-morala, accessed on 15 August 2018; Cartografierea Bucureștiului, Scoala Națională de Studii Politice și Administrative, Departamentul de Sociologie, 2010.

Mircea Vulcănescu, in turn influenced by Alexander Chayanov[77] (see Figure 1). According to a generic peasant work ethic, one has to strive to have enough for the household. The Protestant/capitalist work ethic calls one to strive to have more for oneself and to expand the enterprise. *Enough* and *more* are the two measures of what one *is* more often than of what one *has*. The Romanian word *"îndestulare"* (having enough for your needs and aspirations) differs from *"bunăstare"* (welfare). Of course, what constitutes "enough" (*destul*) is changing, but as far as the peasant ethics of the "good householder" operates, its limits are always established by a shared common sense of the community of belonging. Fundamental societal developments might change it dramatically, as happened during post-communism. After 1989, the rural and/or communist "enough" was no longer sufficient, and therefore people felt betrayed and their dignity as "good workers" was injured. They became the socio-economic losers of transition, and more importantly, its moral losers.

We inherited from this peasant kind of work ethic the moral sense of "enough," which is skeptical about, if not totally opposed to, the notion of "development." For development is never about "enough," it's about more. This is why rural development projects were initially so difficult to implement. The other side of the coin is the reactive excess of "more," which haunted Romanians long after the fall of communism, fueling a "market of desire" and more than enough "conspicuous consumption."

Figure 1:   Peasant vs. capitalist work ethics

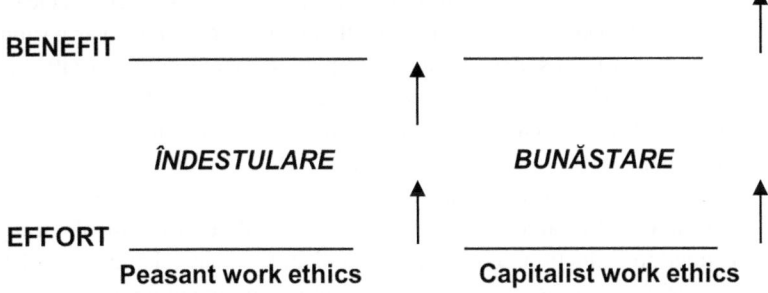

---

77   Mircea Vulcănescu, *Teoria şi sociologia vieţii economice. Prolegomene la studiul morfologiei economice a unui sat* (Bucharest: Eminescu, 1932/1997), 148–166.

The Two Romanias

A hundred years ago, on 25 August 1918, the following dispute took place in the Romanian parliament:
- D.D. Pătrășcanu: This country is a country of peasants!
- D. Stoianovici: Who said this? Where is it written?
- D. Dinu Arion: Romania survived only thanks to the boyars!
- D.I. Teodorescu: It is not true! (great noise, violent protests by the Majority)
- D.P. Greceanu, Vice-president of the Chamber: Gentlemen, you are discussing the issue passionately...[78]

During this time, the peasant was imagined in a Janus-face way. The invisible peasants were pushed to the front stage by the nation-building process and became *the People*; as Liviu Rebreanu pleaded in front of the Romanian Academy in 1940 "the peasant has no name because he is not a class, nor a guild or a profession, but the people itself, the Romanian man."[79] It was in this "popular culture" of the peasantry that the national urban elites searched for arguments for Romanian unity and continuity. From this beginning, the peasant has been viewed paradoxically: he was the bearer of a good *culture*, but a member of a backward *society*. He was born a poet, not an artisan, worker or fighter – and I don't believe that Alecsandri's famous "country brand" ("The Romanian is born poet") was a poetic fantasy. A lasting icon of the nation with which we can identify, the peasant went on functioning as that primitive Other onto which the dominant society could reflect both its aspirations and frustrations.

The expression "the two Romanians," launched by Mircea Vulcănescu in 1932, echoed the still passionate debates of the interwar period. It was meant not as a symbolic geography of upper and lower citizens, but as a search for the best development strategy that Romania could and should follow; Vulcănescu was inclined to bet on the peasant path more than on the urban capitalist way.[80] Despite the communist regime's official claims of solidarity with the poor peasants, the Romanian peasantry was treated as a backward, conservative Other, ideologically destined to extinction. But one has to look at the political and the social-practical faces of the system: communism was a time of forced industri-

---

78 D. Pătrașcu, *In fața națiunii* (Bucharest: Editura Librăriei H. Steiberg & Fiu, 1925).
79 Liviu Rebreanu, *Lauda țaranului român: discurs de recepție la Academia Română rostit în ziua de 29 mai 1940* (Bucharest: Eikon, 1940/2009).
80 Ionuț Butoi, "'Cele două Românii': originile și contextul unei formule controversate," *Sociologie Românească*, XII, 1–2 (2014), 18–31.

alization, but also of "domestication of industry," "etatization of time," privatization of time, theft and counter-theft relations between state and individuals.[81] The post-1989 "transition" was two-fold. Vladimir Pasti identifies an externally-oriented transition, essentially urban, aiming at adapting Romania to the *capitalist* market.[82] Another transition, mainly rural, lacked any internally-driven strategies and coherent reforms, allowed only for underdevelopment, and was a transition from socialism to *feudalism*, as Katherine Verdery put it.[83] The economic and social gap between these two Romanias, between large cities and the rural areas, has increased ever since.

There are no clear borders between these two Romanias, but the tensions between the two imagined communities were worsened by politicization. It started with president Ion Iliescu, a former communist nomenclatura member, who convinced the rural masses and provincial working classes that the King, Corneliu Coposu (the leader of the Peasants' Party) and their boyars wanted to take back their former properties from "the people." Afterwards, the two Romanias were framed as a grand division between the urban educated cosmopolitans and the rural under-educated population, who are suspicious of each other, if not despising each other. Then, we entered democracy through God: "Mr. President, do you believe in God?," Emil Constantinescu asked Iliescu in the 1996 election campaign. It was a smart political move, which soon proved that the Orthodoxy of Constantinescu and the urban conservative elites had little in common with the popular orthopraxy. Religion became a new conflict line between the enlightened cities and the "primitive" countryside. Later, with the emergence of a new, young and urban middle class, a generic countryside Other was seen as the culprit for Romania's lagging development; the generic peasants were an obstacle to the legitimate aspirations of the (new) bourgeoisie. It was the time of "*ciumpalaci*," "monkeys," and other despising categorizations of the rural-cum-elder population. Recently, at the call of the political majority,

---

81 Gerhard Creed, "Agriculture and Domestication of Industry in Rural Bulgaria," *American Ethnologist*, 22, 3 (1995), 528–548; Katherine Verdery, *What Was Socialism, and What Comes Next?* (Princeton: Princeton University Press, 1996); Adriana Oprescu, "Donner, vivre et voler le temps. Les enjeux politiques de la gestion du temps dans la Roumanie des années '80," *Yearbook of the Romanian Society of Cultural Anthropology*, 2 (1999), 21–50.
82 Vladimir Pasti, *România în tranziție. Căderea în viitor* (Bucharest: Nemira, 1995); Vladimir Pasti, "Gradele de libertate ale postcomunismului românesc," *România după douăzeci de ani*, ed. by Vasile Boari, Natalia Vlas și Radu Murea, vol. II (Iasi: Institutul European, 2011).
83 Verdery, *What Was Socialism, and What Comes Next?*

some of this despised population took revenge and openly despised the despisers; it is the time of the "rats," as they called the urban and cosmopolite elites. A strange struggle without classes is waged.

Conclusion

Romania is a post-peasant society where the "agrarian/peasant issue" is still more unresolved than just the post-communist one. In fact, the issue has even stopped being considered a public issue any longer, even if its structural footprint is still considerable. Romania is now a society where, after the "death of the peasant," *The Peasant* is still "spoken" and his heritage is squeezed out either in *aesthetics* (his beautiful culture), or in *ethics* (his bad manners), but almost never approached as a normal *social* process.

Notes on a Century of Surveillance

Katherine Verdery

Abstract: *The formation of Greater Romania in December 1918 entailed building up its intelligence apparatus, both foreign and internal—a development crucial to its survival in the twentieth-century system of national states. Events during the war and provisions of the peace treaty lent special urgency to this development, for the rise of the communist movement in Russia posed grave problems for Romania's eastern border (regularly breached by both refugees and communist agents), and revisions of the border with Hungary increased the threat of Hungarian irredentism. The intelligence services were once again challenged by World War II and the communist takeover; the events of 1989 repeated these challenges. To examine this series of transformations is to ask, among other things, what it means for the form of the state or its ruling regime to change. The paper, delivered as a keynote address at the 2018 international conference organized by the Society for Romanian Studies in Bucharest, explores continuities across these various transitions.*

1 December 2018 marks 100 years since the formation of the unified Romanian state, România Mare or Greater Romania. Such an anniversary invites many possible responses: celebration, revisiting the events of 1918, reassessing or even critically revising how we understand the creation of modern Romania. All these options are open to anyone who loves Romania (as I do).

In this article I explore some transformations undergone by Romania's intelligence services, essential to the survival of the new state in the twentieth century. The topic emerges from a decade of work in the archives of the Securitate (CNSAS), beginning with my own surveillance file. This work has not made me an expert—far from it—but has aroused my curiosity about surveillance in Romania's history. I offer some preliminary notes on this theme, looking briefly at connections among several secret services: those of interwar Romania including the Siguranța and SSI, the communist Securitate, and briefly the SRI after 1989. In part, I consider what revolutionary change in state forms might mean, attending to continuities in the apparatus of self-defense that enabled something called "Romania" to endure for this century.

For this topic as well as many others, Romania should mark not one crucial centenary but two: in 1918 it expanded and unified its territory as a national state, but a year before that, in 1917, the Bolshevik revolution overtook Romania's eastern neighbor. That revolution transformed Russian society beyond recognition and would prove consequential for Romania's future in many respects. The intersection of Marea Unire with the Bolshevik revolution profoundly affected the development of Romania's security apparatus following World War II, and not just for the obvious reason of the KGB's influence. In a word, I believe it makes little sense to commemorate Marea Unire of 1918 without examining its intertwined effects with that other centenary, of Bolshevism.

Preliminaries

My goal is to use the history of the secret police to make a couple of points about analytic methods, relevant to thinking about centenaries in general and the Romanian one in particular. To think about them is to think about *time* in a certain way, as something possessing linear properties based on a progressive sequence of events and dates. Time begins here and travels in a straight line to there, in this mode of thinking. A centenary presupposes that the object moving from Time 1 to Time 2 has a transhistorical core reality—that Romania in 1918 is somehow "the same thing" as Romania in 2018. But is it?

Likewise, we tend to understand revolutionary events as *moments* in time—1 December 1918; 23 August 1944; the abdication of King Michael on 30 December 1947; the execution of the Ceausescus on 25 December 1989—that abruptly changed society's direction. Nevertheless, in actuality they are more protracted and complex than this punctuated representation would suggest. For example, U.S. anthropologist Martha Lampland demonstrates in her recent book, *The Value of Labor: The Science of Commodification in Hungary, 1920-1956*, that Hungarian economists were developing the bases for socialist work norms well before the communist takeover of Hungary.[1] The science and economics of labor, far from being "revolutionized" after 1945 in a new communist state, was part of a continuous movement of thought that served multiple ends before and after the war. To peg it to a particular year so as to celebrate its centenary would make little sense.

---

1   Martha Lampland, *The Value of Labor: The Science of Commodification in Hungary, 1920-1956* (Chicago: University of Chicago Press, 2017).

Such questions about how ideas and events bleed into one another are important to some of the points I will explore below. Among other things I ask about transitions among state forms: how do we know when a state is "the same as" or "different from" one of 25 or 100 years before, particularly when events have taken place that claim to have revolutionized the old order? The answer to that question will affect whether we can even speak of Romania's centenary—a single state existing across a century, even if in different forms. I suggest that looking for continuities rather than ruptures or revolutionary changes facilitates our doing so.

Finally, I should make clear my own relation to the subject of secret police. As is well known, police have been a central feature of modern states since at least the seventeenth century. This police generally includes both the visible police forces that maintain public order and the secret police that work to discover and control hidden information. Given persistent rivalry among states—that is, given a competitive interstate system—each state also maintains usually-secret intelligence forces to help them know what their neighbors and rivals are doing. Thus, the secret police have both internal and international tasks to perform. How they behave is variable: some treat the local population cruelly, others less so—and their treatment can change over time.

I do not contest the necessity of intelligence services in our modern world, though I can find their specific actions more or less distressing. For example, on the basis of my personal experience, evidence, and reading, I can say that I understand why Romania needed a Securitate after World War II, but I condemn some of its actions, or some of the actions of specific Securitate officers. I refer particularly to the period from about 1948 up to the mid-1960s, when the Securitate behaved with excessive brutality against many Romanian citizens. Although things began to improve around 1970, the Securitate was still capable of brutal treatment right up to the end, if less frequently—as dissident engineer and poet Gheorghe Ursu would be the first to tell us, were he still alive.

In the rest of my comments I will refer to several aspects of Romania's national-state formation, particularly the development and transformation of its intelligence services. What I have learned so far from my reading about the secret police in the development of the Romanian national state may not be surprising to my readers but it was to me (evidence, perhaps, of my defective historical understanding). I will use it to question both the dominant view of the national history and the notion of revolutionary change. In saying this, I do not at all wish to deny that for many Romanians of the day, as well as now, unification into a single state was a long-held dream. I will simply try to complicate the field of ideas surrounding that fact.

The Formation of the Siguranța and SSI (Serviciu Special [or Secret] de Informație)

I begin with the formation of the pre-communist secret police, of which the Siguranța and the SSI were the most significant. These organizations underwent repeated changes (including of their names) in the years between Romania's founding in 1859 and World War II. The military intelligence services formed by Alexandru Ioan Cuza were initially trained by French officers, replaced by Prussians after the arrival of King Carol I.[2] As of 1862, writes Vlad Georgescu, the government of the newly conjoined Romanian Principalities had only eight ministries, of which one (domestic affairs) included a general police force, but it was a weak ministry and "had no repressive function."[3] Thirty years later, in 1892, a law created within the Ministry of the Interior a security police under the Direcția Administrației Generale a Personalului și Poliției de Siguranța, or Siguranța Generală. Its jobs included maintaining public order, expelling persons considered dangerous, monitoring foreigners, coordinating a police force, and so on.

Along general lines, this organization continued until 23 August 1944, but the Siguranța Generală itself was thoroughly reorganized in 1908, following the peasant rebellion of 1907 and an attempt on the life of Ion I. C. Brătianu two years later. Politicians realized that had there been a better intelligence organization, the peasant revolt might have been contained; modernizing the police and extending their reach beyond the cities into the villages became a priority. Pavel Moraru writes that the amplitude of the revolt was from "the lack of a central organ of information with specialized antennae spread all across Romania, that would have fulfilled both informative and counterinformative aims."[4] Before the revolt, owing to lack of

---

2   Alin Spânu, *Serviciul de informații al României în Războiul de Întregire Națională (1916–1920)* (Bucharest: Editura Militară, 2012), 16.
3   Vlad Georgescu, *The Romanians: A History* (Columbus: Ohio State University Press, 1991), 139.
4   Pavel Moraru, *La hotarul românesc al Europei: Din istoria Siguranței generale în Basarabia, 1918–1940* (Bucharest: Institutul Național pentru Studiul Totalitarismului, 2008), 24.

information about peasant sentiments, the county prefects had begun using their own funds to organize local information services and hiring their own secret agents. Building up a state security police would preempt these local actions. Now, for the first time, Romania had a state security police (*poliția de siguranța de stat*), with branches all across Romania as well as abroad. A special trait of these information officers was that they no longer depended on county prefects and were organized separately from the rest of the police.[5]

The years between the two wars saw a process of rebuilding and extending the country's security architecture, along with other state structures, to manage an expanded territory and population after 1918. In 1919 the budget of the Siguranța was increased, as the organization was gradually extended into Bucovina, Basarabia (Bessarabia), and Transylvania. The main motivation for reorganizing and enlarging the Siguranța was, of course, that the peace treaty of 1918/20 had altered the country's borders, transferring Basarabia and Bucovina, with their sizable minorities of Slavic-speaking people, from Habsburg or Russian to Romanian control, and transferring Transylvania, with its large population of Hungarians and Germans, to Romania from Hungary. There were not enough Romanian personnel for all the new administrative positions. Indeed, in 1919 some offices of the Siguranța complained that they did not have sufficient Romanian employees for their administration and were having to rely on Hungarians who spoke no Romanian; similarly in Basarabia, where the problem was that the same old German-speaking functionaries from the Austro-Hungarian empire were applying the same old laws as before, waiting for the old order to return.[6] Thus, Romania's expansion created serious problems for governing it. Members of national minorities in both west and east had voted against the union with Romania and would have to be watched closely, lest irredentist forces attempt to revise the borders or Bolshevik agitation threaten stability in Basarabia.

The first reorganization took place in 1922. New procedures included the use of informers and of officers working undercover—two hallmarks of the Romanian Securitate thirty years later.[7] According to

---

5   Ibid., 27.
6   Alin Spânu, *Istoria serviciilor de informații/contrainformații românești în perioada 1919–1945* (Iași: Casa Editorială Demiurg, 2010), 79, 82, 88.
7   An important difference was that whereas the Securitate kept files on both informers and targets of surveillance, the earlier Siguranța did not keep files on informers: it protected its informer network much better than the later

Alin Spânu in his detailed history of the secret services, between 1919 and 1929 the older structures of the DGSP were mainly consolidated and repaired, but a new semi-independent security actor was also being created: the Secret Information Service, or SSI. It was to be instrumental in policing subversion and revisionist actions from the new territories, and it required greater cooperation and data exchange among branches than before. Among its tasks were continuous observation of all social manifestations of any kind and following communists and minority questions up close, even in neighboring countries.[8]

The Bolshevik Revolution, which had turned the territory of Basarabia into a hotbed of Bolshevik anarchy, had complicated Romania's situation greatly.[9] Bolshevik agents poured over the border into Basarabia to organize a Bolshevik movement and to foment instability. Between 1919 and 1925, Russian spy services organized 712 terrorist actions in Basarabia. This meant that the secret services bore a special burden from Romania's unification. The new police and security forces had to keep up with communist organizing there, for parts of the territory remained overtly hostile to the Romanian state. A particularly important section of the Siguranța was dedicated to supervising the communist movement, both in Basarabia and in other Romanian territories; fierce rivalry emerged between this section and the army intelligence division. On the Eastern front, the work of the secret services included identifying not only suspects who crossed the frontier but also refugees from Ukraine, since both were channels for Bolshevik agents to enter Romania. The chaos produced by the incoming refugees would later worsen with the 1930s famine in Ukraine.

Meanwhile, Bolshevik subversion spread. It aimed to stir up popular discontent against the government in Bucharest and to demoralize the Basarabians, alienating them from the Romanian state while also undermining state institutions like the post office and railway. Communist agents kept up a constant barrage of negative propaganda and disinformation, depicting the Siguranța as barbarians, incompetents, and torturers. Soviet publications reveal the image that Soviet propaganda was creating of the Siguranța, quite different from its earlier

---

Securitate would do. See Cristian Troncotă, *Istoria serviciilor secrete românești de la Cuza la Ceaușescu* (Bucharest: Editura 'Ion Cristoiu' S.A., 1999), 356–58.

8   Spânu, *Istoria serviciilor*, 615–6. See also Mircea Vâlcu-Mehedinți, *Dezvăluiri: Fața necunoscută a istoriei României*, Vol. 2., Armata, Veteranii, Siguranța statuluii, Poliția, Jandarmeria (Bucharest: Ed. Mircea Vâlcu-Mehedinți, 2008), 182–5.

9   Spânu provides further information about the effects of Bolshevism in this period (*Serviciul*, 113–115, 165–69).

one: "The image of an odious institution, which fights against the communist movement using the most perfidious methods."[10]

It is clear, then, that on the Eastern Front, the Bolshevik revolution and Romania's unification had created conditions that enhanced the presence and power of the secret services. If we start with 1918, we might miss that possibility. That is, the *conjunction* of the years 1917 and 1918 created fertile ground for the growth of a secret police. My view of this parallels that of Stelian Tănase for the period after 1948, when he argues that the strength and capacity of the early communist secret police organizations (such as the East German Stasi and Romanian Securitate) did not *antedate* the major tasks assigned to them— collectivization, the verification of Party members, or the deportation of the *chiaburs*. Rather, these organizations were *formed_with and by* those tasks.[11] So also, I argue, did the strength and capacity of the Siguranța and SSI grow as a function of their pursuit of communist spies and agitators crossing the Russian border into Basarabia.

In sum, the Bolshevik revolution of 1917 introduced a chaotic situation for Basarabia, with armed incursions, people flowing back and forth, and so on. Security organs developed not simply from the incorporation of new territories but in connection with trying to keep on top of this flux and chaos. I suggest, thus, that acquiring Basarabia made Romania more vulnerable to the Russian revolution—i.e., the cost of getting Basarabia into România Mare was heightened exposure to Bolshevik activity, and this in turn strengthened the secret services. Likewise on the new *western* border: the cost of incorporating Transylvania was Hungarian irredentism that persisted for many years and further strengthened the secret services who had to contain it. Thus, a key aspect of 1918 (expansion of Romania's national territory) entailed developing its security organs. The significance of this growth will become apparent later.

Interwar Secret Services

Romania's efforts to strengthen its security services were badly hit by the Great Depression, which caused budget reductions that eliminated some 2,000 functionaries. Throughout the 1930s these services had to cope with the growth of both the communist party and the extreme

---

10   Moraru, *La hotarul românesc*, 333.
11   Stelian Tănase, *Elite și societate: Guvernarea Gheorghiu-Dej, 1948–1965* (Bucharest: Humanitas, 1998), 50.

right. In this work, the role of the SSI increased while that of the DGP and Siguranța declined, particularly under the royal dictatorship of 1938–40. During those years the SSI outstripped the Siguranta and went from being a department to becoming an independent institution.[12]

The next decade saw organizational changes and the passage of new laws for police operations, creating new organizations for the intelligence services. Under the royal dictatorship the power of these organizations within the state was greatly increased.[13] By 1940 the situation had deteriorated, with the loss of Basarabia to the Soviet Union, Carol II's abdication, and the increasing political presence of extremist groups such as the Legionary movement. Emphasis shifted to counterintelligence so as to catch subversive actions against state security; these included Soviet attacks on Romania through illegal entry, propaganda, spying, and sabotage, which aimed to destroy order by getting Romanian communists to simulate internal conflict. In 1940 a new organization joined the fray, the Legionary Police, which doubled functionaries of the General Directorate of Police. It had its own network of agents that aimed to penetrate institutions and identify enemies of the legionary movement. In 1941 a total reorganization of the DGP took place. Corps of recruiters were created to obtain more informers, but there were still not enough of them.

Then in 1942 the Antonescu government reorganized the security services yet again, strengthening the SSI with the best specialists from the previous organizations of the security police. Thereafter, the SSI consolidated its supremacy in Romania's intelligence landscape and continued its actions against Hungarian irredentism. Following the 23 August coup in 1944, the intelligence services were reorganized yet again and taken over by the communists, who purged them and reduced the police by over 50 percent.[14] At the same time, Spânu writes, in 1945 a number of functionaries who had been fired earlier were verified and rehired. "In 1947, the *efectiv* of the DGP reached 9,339, of which 5,615 (60%) were '*din vechile cadre polițenesti*'," only 3,724 having been hired new.[15] The most important branch of the DGP was the Direcția de Poliție de Siguranța, which had the most numerous and difficult tasks. Its main job was informing, especially concerning the *starea de spirit* of workers and peasants. But repeated purges, reorganizations, and arrests of

---

12 Spânu, *Istoria serviciilor*, 240.
13 Ibid., 615.
14 Ibid., 571.
15 Ibid., 575–6.

higher officers as "a band of agents of the Siguranța" handicapped this effort.¹⁶

By the end of 1947 the communist takeover was complete. A main goal of the new government was to restructure the SSI. In 1948 a Direcția Generală a Securității Statului (DGSS) was formed with Soviet guidance, and in 1951 it swallowed up the SSI, which was disbanded and incorporated into the information structures of the new Securitate.

The Communist "Revolution"

Among the significant problems faced by any large-scale change in the system of rule (that is, not simply a change in the party of government within a parliamentary democracy) is for the new regime to find the staff it requires in order to govern. That is particularly true of the police, armed forces, intelligence services, and bureaucracy. Cristian Troncotă writes:

> The communist revolution would have to create its own armed fist (*brațul înarmat*), the shield that would defend it. The brain of the revolution, however, was aware that this armed fist could not be formed overnight. This is why in Romania, between 23 August 1944 and 30 August 1948, the apparatus of the Siguranța and Special Services did not suffer spectacular organizational modifications except for placing some trustworthy people in leading positions. 'Before creating a party and state', comments Belu Zilber, 'a police was made composed of several police. The former Siguranța Generală made arrests, the prefecture of the police of the capital made arrests, the various services of the NKVD made arrests, the Serviciul Secret de Informații made arrests.'¹⁷

In addition, a verification/purge in the early 1960s found that among the Securitate's officers and subofficers there were 300 former legionaries: the previous purge had not touched the Romanian officers of the Securitate who had a legionary past. Troncotă finds only one possible explanation for this: that top Party officials (with the agreement, one presumes, of the Soviet councilors) believed the radical spirit of the legionaries would be useful in cleansing the rottenness from Romanian politics. The same continuity happened in Hungary, which suggests even more strongly that the Soviets supported the plan. Troncota's conclusion: "In essence we can affirm that the cadre politics promoted in the Securitate at its beginnings had as a consequence a series of black illegalities, reckless acts, and opportunisms. It is a possible explanation, among others, for why precisely in that period we

---

16 Ibid., 587.
17 Troncotă, *Istoria serviciilor secrete românești*, 319–320.

find the most savage measures of repression and state-imposed terror."[18]

Let me repeat this conclusion, in different words: Who got into the new Securitate? At first, people from the former secret services [i.e., the Siguranța and SSI], particularly those of modest social origins or leftist sentiments.[19] In a conference presentation, Spânu details the sequence from 1944–48, known as the period of cohabitation. It began with a decapitation of departments and a vetting of senior officers. As soon as Petru Groza became Prime Minister in 1945 he invited in former Siguranța officers to deal with the members and heads of the historical political parties. Some also served as professors for preparing new officers. Then those who had been specializing in communists and the Soviet Union were arrested, but those doing important work on Hungarian irredentism and legionaries were kept, in part to reconstitute the agentura of before. Gradually even these officers were placed under surveillance or arrested, by 1949. Only in 1969, however, was the dossier concerning former cadres of repression finally closed.[20]

In other words, the communist "revolution" in Romania did not produce a complete rupture of the line of development hitherto: interwar Romania lived on in the new security police.[21] Older Siguranța officers remained in place alongside the new Securitate recruits, whom they would help to train. For the Party, retaining Siguranța officers (as well as former legionaries) might prevent their being recruited by western powers or becoming an underground opposition that the Party would have to deal with.[22] And those Siguranța and SSI officers had skills that new Securitate recruits needed to learn. Coopting them would be preferable to letting them roam the country.

I find in this a possible account of the Securitate's early reputation. In conversation with a Romanian historian, we speculated that perhaps the Siguranța and SSI officers taken into the Securitate were motivated to be seen as more zealous than their colleagues, showing excessive obedience to the Party because of their "bourgeois" past, or perhaps

---

18   Ibid., 339–341.
19   Dumitru Iancu Tăbăcaru, *Sindromul Securității* (Bucharest: Editura PACO, n.d.), 132.
20   Alin Spânu, "Neutralizarea foștilor funcționari din serviciile de informație" (26 September 2013), available at: http://www.youtube.com/watch?v=ZK04Xc6w8sI, accessed 13 August 2018.
21   And in the army and bureaucracy, but that is another story.
22   See Gail Kligman and Katherine Verdery, *Peasants under Siege: The Collectivization of Romanian Agriculture, 1949-1962* (Princeton, NJ: Princeton University Press, 2011), 214.

competing with their new Securitate colleagues by showing they could be even tougher than the others. This possibility differs not only from Troncotă's explanation but also from one I have heard many times in Romania: that the early Securitate was brutal because of the numbers of Hungarian, Jewish, and Russian officers in their ranks. Once those numbers went down, the violence diminished. Although there may be something to this rather chauvinistic explanation, I find it unlikely that Romanian officers (or any other kind, for that matter) were incapable of brutality. I prefer to imagine that in the context of a highly masculine institution, rooted in rural values and competitive violence, the former Siguranța officers vulnerable to being purged would seek to outperform their "brothers" and impress their bosses with their harsh execution of orders. This, in turn, might have colored the culture of the Securitate for some time thereafter. It is unlikely that the influence of KGB councilors would have improved that culture.

This possibility encourages us to reconsider the "rupture" we might think the coming of communism represents. The takeover of Romania by the communist party is usually dated to the period 1945–1948, culminating in the abdication of King Michael at the end of December 1947. The party was getting its personnel into place in different ministries during those three years but did not itself have sufficient numbers to fill all the positions necessary for the state to function. In 1944 it was said to have 1,000 members; within four years that number had increased to 1,000,000, though one suspects that many of them were not convinced communists but rather people trying to feed their families. Although the fraternal help of the Soviet Union doubtless enabled a faster transformation than would have been possible otherwise, many problems would still have to be resolved and many new personnel trained to do so. Former Siguranța officers might do that nicely. As for the Party bureaucracy, a standard-form personnel questionnaire sent out to county functionaries includes two columns, one labeled "cadres needed," and the next—showing smaller figures— "actual cadres."[23] We need no further proof of a personnel shortage.

To step back for a moment, fetishizing dates leads us to see things in terms of ruptures in time—e.g., that Romania before 1918 or 1944 was completely different from Romania in 1920 or 1950. In fact, state apparatuses tend to function with certain continuities, particularly concerning personnel, because they simply cannot train new people fast

---

23 See Kligman and Verdery, Peasants under Siege, 157–158. The example we saw came from Hunedoara county.

enough to replace those of the overthrown *ancien regime*. In this spirit, I recall a remark by Cluj historian Pompiliu Teodor sometime in the early to mid-1990s, observing that his experience of the 1989 "events" and their aftermath had taught him a tremendous amount about how the French Revolution actually took place.

The same questions can be asked about what happened following the "events" of 1989. An article in the *New York Times* for 3 October 1990, for example, reported that Romania's new president, Ion Iliescu, had acknowledged that his government was using "a few thousand" members of the former Securitate to help maintain public order. "The President, Ion Iliescu, insisted in an interview that these officers of the so-called Securitate were people in 'technical functions' who had been screened to establish that they were not guilty of crimes of repression during the dictatorship of Nicolae Ceausescu. Iliescu defended the reemployment of some former Securitate officers indirectly, saying that post-revolutionary Romania had experienced numerous problems in maintaining public order. . . . He said, 'We do not dispose of an efficient service'."[24]

In other words, as had happened in 1945–48, the new *post-communist* state needed reliable cadres for its police and military, and it kept on many of the older ones. A Securitate officer I know—who had himself been kept on for five years after the "events" of '89—said he thought the numbers retained were about 40 percent of the original officer corps, a figure I have seen elsewhere as well. After a time, these officers gradually retired, withdrew, or entered private life, but meanwhile they may have infused into the new SRI some habits from the past.

My own experience is that in 1996, when I returned to do research out in the village of Aurel Vlaicu, three different friends there told me that the Secu officer who had "handled" me before, Col. Iulian Belgiu, had come to ask them what I was doing. I was appalled by this and brought it up in conversation with parliamentary deputy Stelian Tănase, who said I should ask Securitate head Virgil Măgureanu for an audience and an explanation. I did. We met on the steps of the government building in Piața Victoriei, where Măgureanu asked whether I preferred to talk inside or out. When I told him about recent Securitate interference in my village, he replied, "Nu cred că este pe linia noastră." In other words, there were more "linii" then than just the SRI. This was six years after

---

24 David Binder, "Romanians Using the Secret Police," *New York Times*, 4 October 1990, A5.

the revolution. So my conclusion thus far concerning the question of the Romanian state's continuity across the decades from 1918 to 2018 is that if we use developments in the secret police organization, we indeed find continuities that would encourage us to see a single evolving state (and, thus, a centenary).

Other than reading Gheorghe Florescu's revealing book *Confesiunile unui cafegiu* and Marius Oprea's *Moștenitorii Securității*,[25] I know little about what former *securiști* have been doing since December 1989. Aside from those who worked for a few more years in the new SRI, it is rumored that they basically took over Romania's economy, opening security firms, etc. This would make sense: already in Ceausescu's time, *securiștii*—especially in the foreign information service, or DIE, under General Ion Mihai Pacepa—were given the task of helping with Romania's balance of payments by engaging in commerce with state funds. The reason was the lamentable state of the Romanian economy— compared with Hungary, say. As General Neagu Cosma puts it in his book *Cum a fost posibil? Cârtița Pacepa*, "The apparatus of the General Department of External Information was drawn more and more into commercial transactions, finalizing economic contracts, and other activities of external commerce," instead of doing its proper job of gathering intelligence.[26]

Importantly, *securiștii* engaging in these activities made many foreign contacts who would prove invaluable after 1989, once they could work in the open, and they learned a great deal from their foreign business partners about how to run a profitable firm in a capitalist environment. These experiences would give them an advantage in competing with other economic actors. Sometimes their methods were very creative. General Ion Stănescu, the president of the Council of State Security from 1968-72, began a campaign of modernization, and acquired new technology by ingenious methods: he himself stated that he had bought the Securitate's first IBM computer by bartering it for jam.[27]

In sum, we tend to see Romania's transformation from communism in terms of a specific date—25 December 1989. But this

---

25 Gheorghe-Ilie Florescu, *Confesiunile unui cafegiu* (Bucharest: Humanitas, 2008); and Marius Oprea, *Moștenitorii Securității* (Bucharest: Humanitas, 2004).
26 Neagu Cosma, *Cum a fost posibil? Cârtița Pacepa* (București: Editura PACO, n.d.), 150. I realize that it is unwise to take at face value statements from the central actors of the times, but this one seems both plausible and useful.
27 Neagu Cosma and Ion Stanescu, *De la iscoadă la agentul modern: În spionajul și contraspionajul românesc* (București: Editura PACO, 2001), 202.

date signifies little if a great deal of economic activity is in the hands of Securiștii who were already engaged in it for ten to twenty years, if relatively few *ordinary* Romanians have comparable skills, and if the new Security service, the SRI, contains 40 percent of old *securiști* or those closely trained by them.

In a remarkable paper, an East European political scientist takes up this question with actual data too rarely available. Since he chose not to publish his paper after he received a warning from what he assumed was a secret police officer in his home country ("Stop pursuing this subject"), I refer to him as "Anonymous," and I refer to the country he is writing about as "Ruritania," affirming that it offers an appropriate comparison with Romania. "Documents from the archives of the [Ruritanian] State Security," he writes, "as well as in the archives of the [Ruritanian] Communist Party ... allow us to trace the connections between the party, the state, and the secret police both before and after 1989." These documents "reveal the interconnectedness of the party, the state, and the economy both before *and* after the momentous changes of 1989. Tracing these remarkable communist and post-communist continuities allows us to shed new light on the economic and political transformations that took place in Eastern Europe over the last two decades."[28]

He finds that as in Romania, well before 1989 employees of Ruritania's secret police were receiving state funds to create firms both abroad and at home. "Records from the State Security Archive and the Central Party Archive indicate that in the 1960s, State Security was called upon to help the communist state overcome two severe problems: technological backwardness and the shortage of hard currency." As in Romania, Ruritania's External Intelligence Directorate set up import-export businesses abroad, fully owned by State Security, whose employees acquired skills in how to operate in a market economy and could outcompete others lacking this valuable experience. In addition, State Security became an enabler of massive state-supported smuggling operations, first started in 1960 to supply Algerians with weapons. Control over transportation networks and the border became crucial assets. During the 1980s Ruritanian experiments with reform led to private registration of new companies. Through the end of 1989, up to 90 percent of the newly registered companies had a State Security

---

28 Anonymous, "From Spies to Oligarchs: The Party, the State, the Secret Police, and Property Transformations in Post-communist Europe," 4. Manuscript with the author.

connection. "The process of property redistribution [to these secret police]," he states, "had started even before the collapse of communism. Democratization would only accelerate it."[29]

After 1989, top Party officials saw that things were falling apart and, believing that their time was short, they ceded control over most of the Party's valuable assets to people they trusted: the secret police. "Neither the rotation of non-communist parties in government nor entry into the EU has been able to break the monopoly of former employees of the secret police (or their relatives and business partners) over the most desirable assets of the former communist state."[30] The argument is valid, he claims, for all formerly communist countries whose exit from communism was incomplete and where similar processes of redistributing state property to the secret police and their allies could continue without interruption. Eleven countries had a more or less full transformation; in sixteen other countries transformation was incomplete—Romania among them, as well as Russia.[31] In the latter, three successive prime ministers had KGB connections, Putin being the most recent, and after he became president, people with KGB backgrounds began to dominate not just politics but business as well.

*

You are probably thinking, We already know all this: that privatization benefited the old communists. But I am aiming at greater specificity, and Anonymous helps me to provide it. He is not just saying that Party and police, aided by loans from state banks, jointly converted the assets of the Party-state into private businesses. He is specifying that *because* of the economic power accumulated by the secret police *before 1989*, from their activities of trying to shore up failing communist economies there emerged a group of oligarchs rooted in the Security services. Changes in the governing party produced new oligarchs, but these too were rooted in the police.

Anonymous finds that the connection between oligarchs and former secret police is very tight, and that it was the secret police, not the top nomenclatura, who took over the economy. Most of them had a college degree, but in his material the best predictor of oligarch status was a relationship with the Security apparatus. He concludes,

---

29 Ibid., 20.
30 Ibid., 4.
31 Ibid., 27.

Thus, the entire government apparatus in postcommunist [Ruritania] was geared toward enabling business-people with State Security connections to prosper.... It is somewhat paradoxical that State Security, which was designed to serve as the repressive arm of the communist state, would over time become a laboratory for capitalist experimentation.... The [Ruritanian] case amply demonstrates that individuals with State Security connections were the pioneer capitalists before 1989, and that these same individuals then became the most successful post-communist entrepreneurs. Although a new group of oligarchs with no pre-1989 experience as employees or informers of the secret police is emerging, even those oligarchs have benefited from indirect links with State Security. This continuing influence of State Security networks points to the importance of studying communist-era institutions that survived in the post-communist period."[32]

A similar point emerges from Karen Dawisha's 2014 book *Putin's Kleptocracy: Who Owns Russia?*, in which she details the formation of Putin's gang of oligarchs, many of them former KGB or FSB operatives with whom he had worked in St. Petersburg.[33] Sociologist Olga Kryshtanovskaya found that as of 2006, 78 percent of the Russian elite had a KGB connection.[34]

Why should we care about these continuities? As the U.S. Ambassador to Romania said to me sometime in the mid-1990s, "If the economy is being transformed in a capitalist direction, why care if the secret police are behind it? We just want people who have an incentive to develop the rule of law." I have two answers to this: first, the analytical one that urges us to be careful, when we celebrate seemingly "revolutionary" changes in regime, to look for continuity with the prior order so as to trace its effects; and second, the empirical one that despite the early exposure of secret police to market forces, participating in a global capitalist economy will not necessarily turn them into model capitalists. Here I depart somewhat from Anonymous's conclusions. As I learned from my research in the Securitate archives, the secret police developed a subculture and modus operandi with its own rules. The main "rule" governing that subculture is to create chaos, disorder and confusion, beautifully illustrated by Vladimir Putin's foreign policy— such as in Ukraine and Transnistria, for instance—a foreign policy that

---

32 Ibid., 32.
33 Karen Dawisha, *Putin's Kleptocracy: Who Owns Russia?* (New York: Simon and Schuster, 2014).
34 Known as siloviki, this elite was defined as 1,061 individuals who held top positions at the Kremlin, at the regional government, and at the most powerful corporations. Olga Khryshtanovskaya, "Putin's Russia: Kremlin Riddled with Former KGB Agents," *Spiegel Online* (14 December 2006), available at: http://www.spiegel.de/international/putin-s-russia-kremlin-riddled-with-former-kgb-agents-a-454486.html, accessed 24 September 2018.

Dunn and Bobick have called "War Without War and Occupation Without Occupation."³⁵

Vladimir Putin is the most powerful man in the world today, a position he has achieved with the backing of Russia's secret services. He and his allies have proven themselves capable of corrupting the presidential election of the world's most powerful democracy, and they have done that by using standard tricks of the KGB: sow confusion, disinformation, and uncertainty. To me, this does not look like "becoming capitalists," as the US Ambassador expected, but rather more like the final corruption of western/capitalist norms.

If we see the post-communist ascent of the secret police in parts of Eastern Europe and the former Soviet Union as caused by an earlier downturn in the political economies of socialism which they were supposed to fix, should we perhaps also see the collapse of communism as the victory not of a triumphant West but of communist secret police forces across Eastern Europe and Eurasia? The end of communist party rule set loose upon the world a tightly organized corps of secret police having a powerful basis for solidarity, even if in competing factions. As I see it, the legacy of 1989 has been a world-wide mafia-oligarchy consisting not just of former Party apparatchiks but of former intelligence agents from the KGB, the Securitate, and other Eastern European intelligence services, for whom learning capitalist rules may well be less appealing than recasting the economy in their own mold. Are *they* the preeminent experts in internet hacking who are making internet crime the fastest-growing criminal enterprise? Not unlikely. (And we wonder why the world seems to be turning to a "new authoritarianism"...)

*

Let me conclude by recapitulating. After its founding in 1859, Romania's leaders set up an intelligence service that was repeatedly strengthened and reorganized, particularly after the 1907 peasant revolt, and came to be known as the Siguranța. The Bolshevik revolution of 1917 placed severe demands on it to prevent Bolshevik agitation in neighboring Basarabia. The demands were greatly multiplied after Romania's unification the following year, as the new territories of both northern

---

35 Elizabeth Dunn and Michael S. Bobick, "The Empire Strikes Back: War Without War and Occupation Without Occupation in the Russian Sphere of Influence," *American Ethnologist* 41(3) (2014): 405–413.

Transylvania and Basarabia brought in large numbers of ethnic minorities unhappy with the union. From this situation I hypothesize that the security services would be further built up, and indeed after 1918 a new branch was formed, the SSI, specifically to handle these problems. Between 1944 and 1948 the existing organizations were swallowed up in the newly formed Securitate, which retained numbers of the previous officers until an adequate force could be built. I propose that this mingling of personnel affected the culture of the new Securitate, and not in a good way. Likewise, Securitate personnel and practices endured after 1989 in the new SRI, helping to consolidate secret-service dominance in the economy. Wealthy Romanian oligarchs with security backgrounds thus mingle with those of other formerly socialist countries, including Russia, causing us to wonder whether those revolutions ushered in not democracy but a collection of secret-police-inflected mafia states.

I cannot prove most of these assertions: they are hunches. But celebrating the centenary of the Romanian national state includes acknowledging aspects such as these, alongside others worthy of celebration, because self-defense—if it is not excessive—is an essential element of national survival.

Shattered Illusions: Britain and Iuliu Maniu, 1940–1945

Dennis Deletant

Abstract: *During World War II the military situation was never conducive to a defection strategy for Romania. Fear of the Soviet Union had driven Romania into alliance with Nazi Germany and the threat posed by the former continued to cast a shadow over the British Government's efforts to persuade Romania's leaders to steer the country to abandon the Axis. For the British, Iuliu Maniu, the leader of the National Peasant Party, was the pivotal point for any action against the regime of Ion Antonescu. This article uses documents from the British Foreign Office and the British Special Operations Executive (SOE) to trace the British perception of Maniu in 1940–1945, and the steps taken by the Foreign Office and the SOE to maintain contact with him and to encourage him to bring about the overthrow of Antonescu.*

Britain did not have a distinct policy towards Romania during World War II. Following Britain's declaration of war on Romania of 7 December 1941, broader considerations of relations with its new ally, the Soviet Union, dictated British policy towards Marshal Ion Antonescu.[1] The defeat of the Axis powers and, as a prequisite for this goal, the preservation of Allied unity, became paramount considerations for Churchill and Roosevelt and remained so throughout the war. In Whitehall there was little sympathy and sensitivity to the fact that Romania had been driven into alliance with Nazi Germany by fear of the Soviet Union. "Nothing could put Romania on Germany's side," remarked a member of the Romanian Foreign Ministry to the British Minister Sir

---

1   The United States remained neutral until the declaration of war on Japan following the attack on Pearl Harbor on 7 December 1941. Germany declared war on the United States on 11 December, while the United States declared war upon Germany hours later. Romania declared war on the United States on 12 December 1941. On 6 June 1942 the United States declared war on Romania, Hungary and Bulgaria, apparently to establish belligerency status and to ensure that the prisoners of war conventions were operative six days later when thirteen B-24s under Colonel A. Halverson made the first American bombing raid of the war on Ploiești. Ernest H. Latham Jr., ed., *Timeless and Transitory. 20th Century Relations Between Romania and the English-Speaking World* (Bucharest: Vremea, 2012), 274.

Reginald Hoare in March 1940, "except the conviction that only Germany could keep the Soviets out of Romania."² That conviction was quick to form after the collapse of France in May 1940, the Soviet seizure from Romania of Bessarabia and northern Bukovina in June, and the loss of northern Transylvania to Hungary under the Vienna Award in late August.

Romania began to figure in British calculations about Hitler's intentions in Central and Eastern Europe after the Anschluss of March 1938. It was generally believed in the War Office that Germany would seek to impose its will on the area before turning its attention towards Western Europe. Given Romania's geographical position, there was little Britain could offer her. The brutal fact of British-Romanian relations was that "Germany is inconveniently in the way: opportunity, proximity of manufacture and the logistics of supply all told in favour of the Third Reich."³ The British concluded that their only weapon against German ambitions in countries which fell into Hitler's orbit were military subversive operations.⁴

Clandestine Operations

In July 1940, a clandestine agency called the Special Operations Executive (SOE) was created on Churchill's orders in London "to set Europe ablaze." The SOE's propaganda side was christened SO(1) and responsibility for subversive operations was given to SO(2), formed from two clandestine sabotage agencies known as Section D and MI(R). SOE's role was to promote sabotage and subversion in enemy occupied territory and to establish a nucleus of trained men tasked with assisting indigenous resistance groups. SO(2)'s actual strength in personnel is unclear. Colonel Laurence Grand was made head of SO(2) and his second-in-command was Charles Hambro. In August 1941, after a dispute with the Ministry of Information and the Foreign Office, the bulk of SO(1) was transferred to the newly created Political Warfare Executive (PWE), under the control of the Foreign Office, where it was amalgamated with parts of the Foreign Publicity Department of the

---

2   Maurice Pearton, "British Policy towards Romania 1939–1941," in *Romania Observed*, eds. Dennis Deletant and Maurice Pearton (Bucharest: Editura Enciclopedică, 1998), 95.
3   Ibid., 66.
4   These subversive operations are analysed in Dennis Deletant, *British Clandestine Activities in Romania during the Second World War* (Basingstoke: Palgrave Macmillan, 2016).

Ministry of Information and the European Section of the BBC. The SOE remained a purely planning and operations organization until it was disbanded in 1946. During this time, the principal focus of its operations was on occupied Europe, but it also operated in North Africa, the Middle East, South Asia and the Far East.

In March 1940, a propaganda division of Section D had been inaugurated under Alfred George Gardyne de Chastelain with H. Paniguian as adviser.[5] "Subversive and anti-German propaganda was prepared, duplicated each in several thousand copies, and distributed in Romania. When the volume of material became too great to handle comfortably by the duplicating process, a printing press was acquired which operated during normal working hours on legitimate printing business and at night printed SO(2) material."[6] Ion Popovici (code-name *Procopius*[7]) became principal collaborator in connection with the printing press which had been obtained with the assistance of Bondi Kalman of the J. Walter Thomson Company, and Max Fischer, a printing and lithographic expert associated with the *Scrisul Românesc* printing press of Craiova (owned by the brother of former Romanian Prime Minister Tătărescu). Both Kalman and Fischer gave their services voluntarily. Until his departure from Romania in 1940 Fischer was responsible for the purchase from various sources of paper and ink. He

---

5   Alfred De Chastelain (1906–1974) studied engineering at the University of London. In 1927, he joined Unirea company in Bucharest. His expertise led to his recruitment by MI(R) in operations to sabotage the oil wells in Ploiești, but attacks by the Iron Guard on the British engineers involved in these plans forced him to leave Romania in October 1940. In 1941, he became SOE head in Istanbul (code symbol D/H13, and designation 'Field Commander Turkey'). Parachuted into Romania in December 1943 as head of the *Autonomous* mission, he was captured and interned in Bucharest until 23 August 1944. He settled in Calgary, Canada where he died. Arhiva Consiliului Național pentru Studierea Arhivelor Securității (henceforth ACNSAS), I 937873, f.1, and The National Archives, Kew, London (henceforth TNA), HS 8/971. Panihuian (SOE code-number DH/25) was the leader of the Armenian community in Romania. TNA, HS 5/821.
6   TNA, "History SOE Romania," HS 7/186, 1.
7   "Early in 1940 at the request of the London office Ion Popovici, well-known under the pseudonym of Procopius, was engaged on a voluntary basis as postbox and cut-out for Jean Kurciusz, one of the leading members of the Polish Secret Service" (TNA, "History SOE Romania," HS 7/186, 1). Born in Bucharest on 20 May 1898, chemical engineer Ion Popovici joined Unirea as head of sales on 5 October 1924, and died in Bucharest in 1946. Arhivele Militare Române Pitești (henceforth AMRP), fond 5465 – Direcția Justiției Militare, file 2218, 21, and ACNSAS I 937873, f.79.

also took delivery of the finished material and handed it over at clandestine meetings with de Chastelain."[8]

In Romania, the attempt to set the country ablaze had been comprehensively extinguished by the failure of operations to blow up the oilwells. SO(2) then turned its attention to building an anti-German resistance in the country. With the consolidation of Romania's alignment with Germany after Antonescu's advent to power in September 1940, SO(2) concentrated on developing contacts with pro-British members of the opposition to Antonescu.

Iuliu Maniu

The pivotal point for any action against the Antonescu regime was Iuliu Maniu, the National Peasant Party leader.[9] A great-nephew of Simion Bărnuțiu, a leader of the 1848 revolutionary movement of Transylvanian Romanians and representative of the Greek-Catholic wing, Maniu graduated in law in Vienna and Budapest. On his return to Transylvania he became a law professor at the Greek-Catholic seminary in Blaj and a legal advisor to the metropolitan bishop. He joined the Romanian National Party of Transylvania whose program focused on the establishment of Transylvanian autonomy and the assertion of Romanian rights commensurate with the Romanians' demographic majority in the province. In 1909, he was elected a deputy in the Hungarian parliament where he advocated for Romanian aspirations. After being called up into the Austro-Hungarian army in 1915, he emerged from military academy with the rank of second lieutenant and was despatched, first to the Russian front, and then to Italy.

As a member of the National Committee of the Romanian National Party he helped to organize the Grand National Assembly of 1 December 1918, which proclaimed the union of Transylvania with Romania. Maniu led the Directory Council that administered Transylvania from 2 December 1918 until 4 April 1920, when the government of the province was handed over to Bucharest. On 9 August 1919, Maniu became President of the National Party and in October 1926, on its merger with the Peasant Party, he became President of the National Peasant Party. In November 1928, he led the party to victory in the

---

8   TNA, "History SOE Romania," HS 7/186, 1.
9   Born on 8 January 1873 in Bădăcin village, Pericei commune, Transylvania. At the time, the village was in Hungary. Maniu died on 5 February 1953 in the Sighet prison, Romania.

general election and served as Prime Minister until June 1930 when Prince Carol returned to Romania. Maniu had supported the return of the prince on condition that he renounced Lupescu, but Carol's unwillingness to do so prompted him to resign on 7 June. His place was taken by George Mironescu who annulled the act excluding Carol from the throne and then resigned himself. Maniu was recalled on 13 June after Carol gave an undertaking to be crowned with his wife Helen. On learning of Lupescu's return to Romania Maniu submitted his resignation once more on 6 October 1930.

In October 1932, Carol turned to Maniu at the height of a grave economic crisis to head the National Peasant Party government after the resignation of Alexandru Vaida-Voievod. Maniu once again set the conditions of June 1930 for his acceptance. He asked Carol to re-marry Queen Helen, rule in the spirit of the 1923 constitution, and dismiss his influential clique of advisers, the 'camarilla'. Carol agreed to the conditions, but had no intention of abiding by them. The result was that Maniu broke off personal relations with the King and resigned in January 1933. At the same time, he stood down as President of the National Peasant Party, but the King's increasingly dictatorial stance led the party to call on Maniu in November 1937 as the champion of constitutional government and he returned to lead the party. To thwart Carol's moves to instal a royal dictatorship Maniu signed an electoral pact with Corneliu Codreanu, head of the Iron Guard, which had the desired effect of defeating the Tătărescu government. However, Carol dissolved the newly elected parliament and instituted a government of his own choice under Octavian Goga. With Carol's suspension of the constitution in February 1938 Maniu's fear of the institution of a royal dictatorship was confirmed. On 30 March, a decree dissolved all political parties and strict political censorship was applied. Maniu's protests to Carol went unheeded and he thus began what was to be a six-year period as head of the democratic opposition in Romania.

Political opposition

We cannot talk about resistance in Romania either to the Antonescu regime, or to his German allies, in the same terms as in the case of France or Yugoslavia. The circumstances of Antonescu's accession to power, his maintenance of Romania's sovereignty during the period of alliance with Germany, and his pursuit of the war against a communist Russia considered a predator, meant that any armed resistance to his rule was viewed by most Romanians as treachery. It followed from retention of sovereignty that a Romanian resistance movement must engage in resistance not against an oocupying power, but in insurrectionary action against its own national government, in conditions of hostility to such a movement itself. The resistance offered was small in scale – there were no organized resistance operations of the kind conducted by the *maquis* in France, or by Mihailovici and Tito in Yugoslavia. Those partisan groups that took to the mountains of Romania in summer 1944 took action not against German troops but against the Red Army which they saw not as their 'liberator' from 'Fascism' but as an instrument of Soviet communism. This is not to dishonour the few Romanians whose anti-Axis convictions led them to undertake clandestine activities in favour of Allied – particularly British – military intelligence, nor the handful of communists who carried out isolated attacks on the Romanian rail network designed to hinder the Axis war effort against the Russians. But there was no major public opposition within Romania to Antonescu's rule, only spasmodic letters of protest from individual Romanians.[10] Resistance, in the Romanian context, meant political opposition.

In September 1940, De Chastelain met Maniu in the house of Rică Georgescu.[11] Plans were discussed for the Peasant Party leader to travel

---

10 The files prepared for Antonescu's trial in May 1946, containing letters of protest addressed to him and seen by this author, run to only a handful of volumes. It is unclear whether the letters, filed by the Romanian Intelligence Service (SSI), ever reached Antonescu's desk. Arhivele Naționale Istorice Centrale (formerly the State Archives, Bucharest, henceforth ANIC), Ministerul Afacerilor Interne, "Trial of Ion Antonescu," file 40010, volumes 35 and 37.

11 TNA, "History of SOE Romania," HS 7/186, 5. Valeriu (Rică) Constantin Simion Georgescu (SOE code-name *Jockey*) was born on 3 February 1904 in Brăila. He studied engineering at University of Birmingham and worked for the Unirea company, where he met de Chastelain, before joining the Român̂o-Americană (Standard Oil) company. With the support of the SOE and Maniu, Georgescu set up a radio link with London in spring 1941. Arrested on 15 August by the Germans and handed over to the Romanian authorities, he was released on 23 August 1944. He served as Under-Secretary of State at the Ministry of Industry, Trade and Mines in 1944, and Director-General of the Român̂o-Americană company in 1944–1946. In 1947, he and his wife left Romania without their two sons to visit the United States and did not return. They became US citizens in 1952. Efforts to persuade the Romanian authorities to allow their children to join them proved unsuccessful until the direct intervention of President Dwight Eisenhower. In 1954, Eisenhower wrote to Gheorghe Gheorghiu-Dej asking him to "expedite a satisfactory solution" (Eisenhower to Gheorghiu-Dej, 25 February 1954, AWF/D. Eisenhower, Dwight D. To Valeriu C. Georgescu, 23 July 1953, in *The Papers of Dwight David Eisenhower*, eds. L. Galambos and D. van Ee, doc. 339 (Baltimore, MD: The Johns Hopkins University Press, 1996), http://www.eisenhowermem

to London to set up a Free Romanian Committee. Maniu agreed and decided that his Committee would consist of Virgil Madgearu, ex-Minister of Finance and a leading economist, Ion Mihalache, Maniu's deputy, Nicolae Titulescu, then in Switzerland, with Carol Davila as his representative in the United States.[12] Unfortunately Madgearu was assassinated by the Iron Guard on 27 November 1940, Titulescu was in poor health and died a natural death at Cannes on 17 March 1941, and Mihalache refused to leave the country. In their place Maniu sent abroad in December Cornel Bianu to replace Madgearu and Ştefan Neniţescu to act as his secretary. "Pavel Pavel also left with the blessing of Maniu but in no way as his representative." Georgescu enlisted the support of his uncle, General Alexander Manolescu, ex-*aide de camp* to Prince Nicholas, and a person well connected in military and Palace circles. "Manolescu also accepted a fund of one million lei to cover entertainment expenses to be incurred in furthering our [SOE's *author's note*] interests."[13]

On 30 September 1940, de Chastelain left Romania on the insistence of Sir Reginald Hoare who was concerned about de Chastelain's safety following the collapse of the plan to sabotage the oilfields. De Chastelain handed over the SOE organisation to Herbert Watts, who became a victim of the rapidly-deteriorating state of British-Romanian relations and was obliged to leave the country within weeks. His role was assumed by R. Hazell, "who until then had been collaborating with the Polish organisation in Romania."[14]

The principal thrust of SOE activity in Romania during this period was provided by the propaganda effort, directed by SO(1), in August 1941 to become the Political Warfare Executive (PWE) – in this respect

---

orial.org/presidential-papers/first-term/documents/339.cfm, accessed on 28 August 2018). Gheorghiu-Dej agreed to the release. The family was reunited in New York City on 13 April 1954. Georgescu died in Switzerland on 31 October 1993.

12 Virgil Madgearu (1887–1940) was a Professor of Economics at the Universty of Bucharest and Finance Minister in the National Peasant Party governments of 1929–1930 and 1932–1933. Ion Mihalache (1882–1963) was a teacher who became a leading figure in the Peasant Party and, after its union with the National Party in 1926, in the National Peasant Party. He served as Minister of Agriculture in the governments of Alexandru Vaida-Voevod and Iuliu Maniu (1919–1920 and 1928–1930), Minister of Internal Affairs (1930–1931 and 1932–1933), and President of the National Peasant Party (1933–1937). Mihalache was arrested with other leading members of the party in 1947, tried for espionage in favour of the United States and Britain, and sentenced to hard labour for life. He died in Râmnicul Sărat prison on 6 March 1963.
13 TNA, "History SOE Romania," HS 7/186, 5.
14 Ibid.

Ion Popovici and Rică Georgescu were the mainstays. Both supervised the work of the printing-press with the help of Max Davidovici, "who was also supplying very valuable military information to the military attaché covering most provinces of Romania."[15] The press produced material for Chalmers-Wright of the Ministry of Information on behalf of *Ardealul*, the first 'black' propaganda radio station set up by SOE in London in October 1940.[16] The station's first team was formed by Robert William Seton-Watson,[17] Viorel Virgil Tilea, the former Romanian Minister to Britain,[18] and Dan Dimăncescu, a former counsellor at the Romanian legation in London.[19] Known variously in British circles as R.1, Romanian Brethren (*Frați Români*), Independent Romania (*România*

---

15 Ibid.
16 The British propaganda campaign in Romania is admirably analysed by Ioannis Stefanidis, *Substitute for Power. Wartime British Propaganda to the Balkans, 1939–44* (Farnham: Ashgate, 2012), 127–159. For this reason, I do not propose to discuss it in detail here.
17 Seton-Watson was born on 20 August 1879. After graduation from Oxford University in 1901, he travelled in Central Europe, focusing his attention upon Hungary which he visited in 1906. His experience there made him a forceful critic of Hungary's policies towards its subject peoples, the Romanians, Slovaks and the Serbs. After writing a number of articles in this vein for *The Spectator* he published in 1908 his first major work, *Racial Problems in Hungary*. His close interest in Central Europe brought him into firm friendship with the Vienna correspondent of *The Times*, Henry Wickham Steed, and with the Czech politician Tomás Masaryk. Defending the *status quo* was a prime aim of Seton-Watson during the inter-war period. As a firm advocate of the territorial integrity of Greater Romania, he became a harsh critic of British Prime Minister Neville Chamberlain's policy of appeasement. After Chamberlain's resignation in 1940, Seton-Watson joined the Foreign Research and Press Service (1939–1940) and then the Political Intelligence Bureau of the Foreign Office (1940–1942). He remained a vocal spokesperson for Romania. Romania's entry into World War II on the side of Nazi Germany in 1941 torpedoed any pro-Romanian influence Seton-Watson sought to bear on British policy. With his hopes of the emergence of a liberal democratic Romania from World War II shattered by the imposition of communism, he retired to the family home in Scotland where he died on 25 July 1951.
18 Viorel Tilea (6 April 1896–20 September 1972) was the Romanian Minister to London during 1938–1940. He was granted political asylum in the United Kingdom in September 1940 after being recalled to Bucharest following Ion Antonescu's accession to power.
19 A graduate of the University of Bucharest, Dimitrie Demetrios Dimancescu (7 July 1896–8 December 1984) received the British Military Cross for sabotaging Romanian oil wells during World War I to hamper the German war effort. After World War I, he studied engineering at the Carnegie Institute of Technology in Pittsburgh. He was counselor at the Romanian legation in London in 1940 when German troops entered Romania, and he then resigned his position. After World War II, he lived in Morocco and then settled in Hartford Connecticut in 1956. Latham, Jr., ed., *Timeless and Transitory*, 397–445.

independentă) was commonly referred to by the Romanian name for Transylvania (*Ardealul*) on account of its cover, an anti-Antonescu group allegedly based in Romania. During its early broadcasts, it was charged with creating an "atmosphere of transmission by Roumanians in Roumania for Roumanians."[20] The principal aims of the station were to dissuade Romanians from supporting military and economic assistance to Germany, to disrupt economic activity, and to encourage opposition to Antonescu and to the Iron Guard. Propaganda on behalf of *Ardealul* was printed by a group coordinated by Ion Popovici, Rică Georgescu and Iosif Păsătoiu, with finance provided by de Chastelain.[21]

De Chastelain returned to Romania on 15 January 1941 and re-established contact with all individuals and organizations then collaborating with SOE. Under Hazell's direction a large war chest had been accumulated and handed over to Popovici to finance Maniu and *Ardealul*. De Chastelain made a second, final, trip to Bucharest after the Iron Guard rebellion of 22–25 January 1941 and reached final agreement with Maniu as to procedure once the British Legation had left the country. By that time the Minister and certain of his secretaries were well informed of SOE's plans, and consequently decisions were taken in agreement with the Minister, SOE and Maniu. Maniu claimed to have made arrangements for an important amount of sabotage which could be put into effect by the end of February. This sabotage was conditional on the bombing by the RAF of oil refineries and certain rail targets in Romania. It was on the understanding that such bombing would be carried out that Sir Reginald Hoare concurred in the breaking of diplomatic relations with Romania.[22] Among the final arrangements made with Maniu was a signal plan for the Wireless Transitter and Receiver (W/T) set which was to provide communications between Bucharest and Istanbul after the departure of the British diplomatic mission. De Chastelain used two visits in January and February to contact the Romanians with whom SO(2) planned to work after the Legation left, principally Maniu, Rică Georgescu, and Ion Popovici.

On 10 February, Hoare informed Antonescu by note that since Romanian territory "was being used by Germany as a military base in furtherance of her plans for prosecuting the war" the British Government had decided to recall him and the diplomatic mission. He

---

20 Stefanidis, *Substitute for Power*, 151.
21 Păsătoiu received 10 million *lei*. AMRP, fond 5465 – Direcția Justiției Militare, file 2218, 24.
22 TNA, "History SOE Romania," HS 7/186, 6.

proposed to leave Romania on 15 February. On the eve of Britain's severance of diplomatic relations Hoare, admitting that 'the game is up', had to agree with Maniu that the National Peasant Party should maintain contact with the British by radio.[23] For almost three years radio and occasional courrier were the means of contact with Romania. A wireless set was left with Valeriu 'Rică' Georgescu and ten million *lei* from the coffers of the British-owned *Unirea* oil company to fund a resistance group of members of Maniu's party.[24] The Minister's final impression was that "though Maniu's intentions are the very best, he is sadly lacking in inspiration......However, there is nobody else who could head a patriotic movement, and so at present it is Maniu or nothing."[25]

Maniu had apparently promised both Hoare and de Chastelain that he, too, would leave shortly afterwards, but he did not and the trickle of messages forwarded by Georgescu gave no reason why. The problems arising from Maniu's indecisiveness were not helped by scheming with Romanian emigré circles in London. Partly out of deference to Maniu the Foreign Office refused to support a Free Romanian Movement in Britain. A second reason was that no other Romanian abroad was considered "of sufficient calibre to command serious [domestic] support."[26] Finally, after June 1941, such a move was expected to dangerously complicate relations with the Soviet Union. Without such an organization, Romanian émigrés were riven by factionalism, thereby reducing their effectiveness as a political group to the Foreign Office and SOE. Viorel Tilea, the former Romanian minister to London, proved to be particularly difficult. In early 1941, Tilea was allowed to establish a Romanian National Committee but the Foreign Office withheld recognition or publicity. Before long, a group of mostly Maniu's supporters broke away and formed a short-lived Romanian Democratic Committee. They considered

---

23 Ivor Porter, *Operation Autonomous: With S.O.E. in Wartime Romania* (London: Chatto and Windus, 1989), 66.
24 The other members were Ion Beza, Iuliu Bălan, Ştefan Cosmovici, Ion Deleanu, Ion Dragu, Mihai Iaroslavici, Iosif Păsătoiu, Ion Popovici, Corneliu Radocea, and Augustin Vişa (author's interview with Corneliu Coposu, 13 August 1986). Bălan, a nephew of Maniu, was head of the Bucharest repair shop at AEG, the German electrical manufacturer, and transmitted messages which were brought to him by Vişa. Popovici, de Chastelain's assistant at *Unirea*, recruited Beza, a wireless operator at the Romanian airline *Lares*. Ibid., 72.
25 Elisabeth Barker, *British Policy in South-East Europe in the Second World War* (London: Macmillan, 1976), 77.
26 Ibid.

Tilea and his associates tainted by their past association with former king Carol.[27]

Radio communication with Maniu

On 8 April 1941, the first message was received from Maniu's W/T set, known as Z.4.[28] It claimed to have been on the air for several weeks before this. Messages continued regularly from Z.4 until 23 June, the day after Germany and Romania attacked Russia. The Romanian contacts proved an invaluable resource, penetrating even into the German High Command in Bucharest. As a consequence, Popovici told London on 11 April 1941 that Germany would attack Russia on 15 June that year. This information was provided by General Alexander Manolescu, Rică Georgescu's uncle, from a source in the German High Command.[29]

Z.4 was used to exchange messages with advice from the British Government over Germany's invitation to Romania to occupy the Serbian Banat. "Maniu, and undoubtedly through him Antonescu, was warned that His Majesty's Government would regard as an enemy any

---

27 Stefanidis, *Substitute for Power*, 156 and 157, footnote 195. This view was confirmed by Lord Glennconner, head of the Cairo Headquarters Directorate of SOE, on 9 February 1942: "We have obtained a copy from New York of a letter from Pangal, ex-Roumanian Minister at Lisbon, to King Carol. This letter, which was intercepted at Bermuda, shows that Pangal is scheming for the return of King Carol, is in communication with Tilea. The Poles have a W/T set in Bucharest and are (presumably) passing messages into Roumania for Tilea. It is therefore probable that there is an intrigue going on between the Poles, Tilea and King Carol, who are opposed to Maniu." TNA, "Minute on Roumania," HS 5/765. Lord Glennconner was Christopher Grey Tennant, 2nd Baron Glenconner, 1899–1983.

28 TNA, "History SOE Romania," HS 7/186, 7. Ivor Porter, in an e-mail sent to this author on 23 May 2008, gave an earlier date: "the first radio contact between Maniu and SOE Istanbul was made on 4 April 1941 with Balan's transmitter. This was hand-made by Balan from components he normally had on his bench. Balan's operation, which lasted until 15 August 1941, was associated with no other transmitter. When I joined SOE in March 1941 I was based in Cairo. Early in 1943 when I visited Istanbul, de Chastelain who was then head of the SOE office told me of his attempts to keep in touch with Maniu after the arrests of August 1941. He talked at length of how he had finally succeeded in sending Maniu an SOE set 'to replace Balan's' via a buccaneering Turk called Lufti Bey. He made no mention of the suitcase set he had left with Georgescu in Romania in 1940 and I probably knew nothing about it. There is no evidence that the 1940 suitcase transmitter was ever used and it was almost certainly the one referred to in SOE papers. Balan's home-made stationary set proved to be a successful stand-by. I agree with your conclusion" that de Chastelain's transmitter was never used.

29 TNA, "History SOE Romania," HS 7/186, 7. A note in this file adds: "The attack took place on 22 June, being delayed a week on account of the signing of the German/Turkish Pact of Friendship."

country which sided with Germany against Soviet Russia. He was also informed by the emigré Yugoslav Government through HMG that the occupation of the Banat would be regarded as an enemy act subject to settlement at the Peace Conference, with inevitable bad effects on Romania' s relations with Yugoslavia."[30] Radio contact with Maniu was broken when both Georgescu and his associates were caught by the Germans on 15 August 1941 and handed over to the Romanians.[31] Those arrested included Popovici, Badica Iaroslavici, Ion Beza (the operator of the W/T set), Iosif Păsătoiu, Ștefan Cosmovici, Alexandru Klamer, Ion Deleanu, Mihai Iaroslavici, Corneliu Radocea, and Augustin Vișa.[32]

In early January 1942 the Foreign Office and the SOE agreed that "Maniu is our best hope of starting an anti-Axis movement" and that "a *coup d'état* would be the goal to aim at"; the implication was that he should therefore stay in Romania.[33] Correspondence in mid-January between Foreign Office officials suggests that Maniu had decided to leave Romania "for British territory," and SOE in Cairo was asked to issue travel documents for the party under English names.[34] Yet Maniu never took up the opportunity. He argued that he had to remain in Romania to lead his party since he was the only person able of doing so. Exile, he claimed, would damage his standing in Romania.[35] Maniu's indecisiveness did not prevent Eden from presenting him to the Russians as the best chance of getting Romania to abandon the Axis. An *aide-mémoire* handed by Eden to Maisky, the Soviet ambassador to London, on 21 March argued that the only person with whom negotiations over Romania's exit from the war could be conducted was

---

30 TNA, "History SOE Romania," HS 7/186, 7.
31 Under questioning during his trial with Ion Antonescu and their associates, Mihai Antonescu stated that the Germans wanted Georgescu to be put on trial but he "did not consider it to be in the Romanians' interest ....because that interest did not require that publicity should be given to a matter of espionage involving Britain at that time.....I intervened [to ensure] that there should never be a trial." *Procesul Mareșalului Antonescu. Documente*, vol.1 (Bucharest: Editura Saeculum, Europa Nova, 1995), 289–90.
32 Born on 15 February 1909 in Bucharest, Ioan Beza was released from prison on 23 August 1944 but was re-arrested by the NKVD on 17 June 1947 and sentenced to 25 years in prison. He served his prison term in the Soviet Union and Gherla, Romania. He died in January 1958. (I am grateful to Ioan Ciupea of the National Musem of History in Cluj-Napoca for these details.) Iosif Păsătoiu was arrested in 1946 for membership of an anti-communist group. He was later interned for 24 months on 20 September 1951.
33 Barker, *British Policy in South-East Europe*, 224.
34 The National Archives HS 5/760, "Tom [codename of Maniu] departure from Romania," telegram from Cairo to SOE in London, 19 January 1942.
35 The National Archives, HS 5/763.

Maniu. Six days later, Eden enquired whether Maisky had received a response, and on 29 April he wrote again. It was only on 15 May that the ambassador told Eden that the Soviet government "did not for the moment want to take any action with M. Maniu."[36]

There was also an absence of positive action on Maniu's part. It was most obvious at the paramilitary level. If the British believed that a 'patriotic movement' headed by Maniu would undertake resistance operations as Mihailovici and Tito in Yugoslavia, then they were to be sorely disappointed. Maniu's inaction in this regard was acutely embarrassing to the Romanian section of SOE. In the eyes of the British Maniu could not be relied upon to make decisions or to give firm directions to his supporters, although he was a perceptive political analyst.[37] A serious obstacle was Maniu's suspicion of Russia's intentions in the event of a German-Romanian defeat. In September 1942, Maniu had communicated his concern to SOE: "so long as we do not know positively....that the allied nations are willing to exclude a Russian invasion of Romania once the German front collapses.....it is practically impossible for our opposition...to come out against the Axis and organize anything with concrete effect."[38] The Foreign Office was unwilling to raise this matter with Moscow, for fear of giving the Russians an opportunity to openly declare their interests in respect of Romania.

By the end of the year, the idea of leaving Romania found favour with Maniu, who also advanced the idea of an Allied (but not Soviet) airborne landing to back up a Romanian *volte-face*. Such overtly anti-Soviet initiatives worried the Foreign Office, which remained convinced that no action regarding Romania should be taken without consulting the Russians, a view which they conveyed to the State Department in January 1943.[39]

The position of the Foreign Office

In a reply to Sir Charles Hambro, head of SOE,[40] Sir Alexander Cadogan, Permanent Under-Secretary at the Foreign Office from January 1938 to

---

36 Barker, *British Policy*, 225.
37 Gheorghe Buzatu, *România și Marile Puteri, 1939–1947* (Bucharest: Editura Enciclopedică, 2003), 548.
38 Barker, *British Policy*, 225.
39 Ibid., 226.
40 Hambro replaced Sir Frank Nelson as SOE head in April 1942. Nelson withdrew as head because of ill health.

February 1946, explained the Foreign Office's position on 31 December 1942:

> The short-term advantages of cooperating with Maniu (i.e sabotage, disruption of the army etc.) are too small and too problematic to justify the long-term disadvantage of committing ourselves in advance with regard to the political and territorial future of Romania. From his messages, it seems clear to us that Maniu is primarily interested not in working out immediate plans for sabotage and mutiny, but in formulating a policy for the future of Romania and in safeguarding as far as possible her position at the eventual peace settlement... He is most anxious to induce us to guarantee the frontiers of Romania against both Hungary and the Soviet Union, and particularly against the latter. Since in the nature of things the Soviet Government has a special interest in Romania, we have always recognized that we cannot adopt a positive policy towards Romania without first consulting the Soviet Government. It was for this purpose that we offered last spring to put the Soviet Government in touch with Maniu. The fact that they declined our offer is, I think, proof that they intend to keep their hands free.

He continued:

> If we now again raise the question with the Soviet Government and put forward definite proposals for the future territorial settlement and government of Romania on the lines desired by Maniu, we shall be making a beginning to which there is no visible end. Once started, these discussions could not possibly be limited to Romania, but would inevitably extend to the post-war settlement of the whole of the Balkans and of Central Europe. When the time comes to discuss these problems with the Soviet Government there will be trouble enough, quite apart from Romania, and it is even possible that in order to get what we want in other respects, we shall have to acquiesce in the Soviet Government's claim to dispose of Romania as they wish, and in order to save the rest of the Balkans, we may even be obliged to throw Romania to the wolves. You will understand, therefore, that it is politically impossible for us at present either to formulate a positive policy with regard to the future of Romania or to tackle the Soviet Government on these lines.
> ....we do not rate the prospects of effective sabotage in Romania very high, nor do we believe that Maniu is in a position to make a really substantial contribution to the war effort. Nevertheless on this point we are prepared to admit that we may be wrong. If Maniu really can bring about the disintegration of the Romanian armies in the Soviet Union, then it would of course be worthwhile paying him a fairly stiff price. In this, however, the Russians are mainly concerned. It is they who will be the chief gainers by such a move and they who will have to pay the price. Theirs must therefore, we think, be the decision. We would propose then, if you see no objection, to pass on to the Soviet Government some of the information contained in your papers and to ask them whether, in the circumstances, they now wish to get in touch with Maniu.[41]

The Foreign Office therefore temporized over a request from Maniu the following month to send representatives to London until they conferred with Moscow. In March 1943, the Russians reacted. Eden, who was

---

41   The National Archives, HS8/957.

visiting Moscow, received a personal letter from Molotov. Whilst declining any contact with Maniu themselves, the Russians supported continued British links: "it is possible that in the course of negotiations a basis may be found for collaboration between this group and the British and Soviet governments."[42]

Operation Ranji

With this green light from Moscow SOE was given authority to prepare missions to Romania. The first was dispatched in June 1943 to work alongside Maniu. Captain Thomas Charles David Augusten Russell MC of the Scots Guards was dropped together with a Romanian wireless operator Nicolae Țurcanu on the night of 15/16 June in Yugoslavia on a mission code-named *Ranji* to Romania. This was the first British-led mission to be despatched by SOE to Romania since it entered the war. The mission's task was to penetrate into Romania for the purposes of "opening-up W/T communications, effecting contact with Maniu's organization, and organizing a reception area in the Romanian Carpathians."[43] The two-man team was dropped to a reception committee arranged by a British mission with Mihailovici's forces in the Homolje area.

This mission to Yugoslavia was led by Captain Jasper Rootham, who described his new colleague thus: "David Russell, tall, fair-haired and blue-eyed, with an infectious smile, instantly won all hearts, not least because he was the Serbs' idea of what an Englishman should look like."[44] Rootham considered Russell's mission "a madcap one" and

---

42 Barker, *British Policy*, 226; Porter, *Operation Autonomous*, 93.
43 A SOE report reference DH 109 [Major E.C. Boxshall, author's note]/RO/169/3 dated 29 July 1943 from D/HV [Lt-Col J.S.A Pearson] stated: "We have received a reply from Cairo to the following effect. Russell was educated at Eton and Cambridge where he took his BA in Agriculture. He was later at Heidelberg and Bonn universities and speaks fluent German. In September 1942 he took part in the raid on Tobruk and, dressed as a German officer, was later responsible for arranging the escape of two officers and eight other ranks from Tobruk for which he was awarded the Military Cross. Russell was parachuted into Yugoslavia on 15 June... to cross into Romania and to establish himself in the Godeanu mountains where he is to arrange a reception area for further British Liaison Officers." The National Archives, HS 5/798.
44 Rootham gave an account of Russell's time with him in Yugoslavia in his wartime memoir, Jasper Rootham, *Miss Fire* (London: Chatto and Windus, 1946), 64.

hazardous.⁴⁵ This opinion was shared by the local Chetnik commander Velja, whose warning was sadly prophetic:

> it would be most unwise for Russell to go only with his wireless operator, and offered to provide a bodyguard of thirty men if we would arm them. There were, he explained, numbers of villages on the Romanian side of the Danube whose inhabitants were Serb; he had contact with them and would be able to organize a sort of base headquarters for Russell from which he could sally forth on his appointed task. Otherwise, said Velja with the utmost seriousness, he would not give much for Russell's chances. He would be murdered by some Rumanian peasant for his money."⁴⁶

The *Ranji* mission, augmented by a Romanian-speaking Serb Chetnik, crossed the Danube into Romania on 2 August. Towards the middle of the month they established themselves in a forest near Vârciorova, where they made contact with the Pitulescu brothers, one of whom was a prominent Peasant Party associate of Maniu, and from where they sent their first W/T messages from Romania on 12 and 13 August. It was in this forest that Captain Russell was murdered on 4 September, probably for the gold sovereigns he was carrying to use as payment. Post-war enquiry never succeeded in establishing by whom he was killed. Țurcanu, who discovered his body, reported his death to SOE in Cairo on 20 September from Bucharest under the code-name *Reginald* using a Royal Navy cipher which he kept on a silk handkerchief.⁴⁷ He had taken shelter at the flat of an old friend, Captain Radu Protopopescu, who obtained false papers for him and told him of friends willing to take action against the Germans in Romania.⁴⁸

---

45 Alan Ogden, *Through Hitler's Back Door. SOE Operations in Hungary, Slovakia, Romania and Bulgaria, 1939–1945* (Barnsley: Pen and Sword, 2010), 242.
46 Rootham, *Miss Fire*, 68.
47 Letter to this author dated 6 July 1984 from Christopher Woods, SOE adviser to the Foreign and Commonwealth Office. Țurcanu, or Vella as he was known when he worked clandestinely in Romania, outlines his wartime experience in the Bucharest daily *Timpul* on 1 October 1944. He was a Bessarabian, bilingual in Romanian and Russian, and had served in the Romanian merchant navy. His ship was in a British port when Britain and Germany declared war, so he transferred to the British merchant navy. He was recruited by SOE, given parachute and wireless training, and the rank of Lieutenant. After arriving in Bucharest in autumn 1943, he began transmissions for Maniu. Contacts in the police warned him whenever German trackers got on his scent but on 10 July 1944 they located him and the Romanian police arrested him. He hid his radio and recovered it after 23 August, using it to communicate with the Americans who sent bombers to attack German positions at Otopeni airfield on 26 August.
48 Among those willing to act were Virgil Tabacu, a police inspector in Bucharest, and Sandu Ioan, an air-force captain. Porter, *Operation Autonomous*, 99–100; Ogden, *Through Hitler's Back Door,* 242–49.

SOE attempts to find the perpetrator could produce no hard evidence against anyone. Word had soon spread of the mission's presence in the area, attracting police and military patrols and several bands of cut-throat thieves including Serbian guerillas. In a US Office of Strategic Services (OSS) report dated 3 November 1944, a source claimed that between 29 August and 19 September 1943, Romanian officials knew about a three-man W/T party. The information was highly accurate: Vella Nicolo Antonio, "a soldier of fortune"; Albert Thomas, "a British or American"; Petre Mihai, "a Serb Chetnik." A forest ranger had reported them, noting that Thomas was in British Army Battledress and Petre Mihai in Romanian peasant costume.[49]

In weekly Progress Report 61 for the week ending on 23 September 1943, the SOE desk officer wrote that Russell "probably undertook one of the most difficult of missions, bearing in mind that Romania is an enemy country and no reception arrangements could be made for him. The result of this mission is that we are now in W/T communication with Romania, which we have been trying to establish for the past two years."[50] Charles St George Maydwell, Russell's Commanding Officer, informed the family.[51]

---

49 "No murder weapon was found. Police reports state that the body was recovered after some days and that the bullet was a 12 mm or .455. But whose gun? When the Mission had stayed with Madgearu, they had allowed him to cache two out of their three .455 revolvers. This is made clear by Russell when he signalled Cairo on 24 August: 'only weapon is one pistol. Please send colt automatic and magazines'." Ogden, *Through Hitler's Back Door*, 245.
50 The National Archives, HS 9/1293/3.
51 On 1 June 1944, Russell was posthumously mentioned in despatches, somewhat ungenerous recognition given the importance of his mission. His father, Captain E.Russell, corresponded with the War office about his grave. His other son, George, had been killed at El Alamein with the 7th Batallion, The Rifle Brigade, but in his case his father visited his grave with its view over the Mediterranean. Russell's grave, a wooden cross at Vârciorova, had been left unmarked since neither the Germans nor the Romanians would have countenanced it. Once the area was under the control of the Allied Commission, a headstone was organised to replace the simple anonymous cross with the inscription "Captain David Russell, a gallant gentleman who died in the battle for the liberty of Europe." His father wondered whether the Military Cross could be added and offered to pay for the cost and upkeep of the grave. The advice of the British Commission was sanguine – "best not as we cannot guarantee that the mayor will use the funds for the purposes you intend." The National Archives, HS4/HS5.

Operation Autonomous

A second SOE mission to Romania had been planned in spring 1943. De Chastelain, the head of SOE in Istanbul, left Turkey for London and in July travelled to Canada to recruit native speakers for missions to Bulgaria, Hungary and Romania. He then went on to Egypt for parachute training in preparation for the mission to Romania, code-named *Autonomous*. Radio contact was maintained through 'Reginald' with Rică Georgescu, who despite being in jail in Bucharest, was given liberal visiting rights by the authorities and was allowed to roam at leisure inside the prison. Originally, the mission had been conceived as a classical operation to disrupt German communications, but Stalin unexpectedly agreed in November that Maniu should be allowed to send an emissary to the Allies to discuss operational details for the overthrow of Antonescu and "its replacement by a Government prepared to surrender unconditionally to the three principal Allies."[52] The Soviet government insisted that a Soviet representative take part in the negotiations. *Autonomous* assumed a predominantly political purpose, de Chastelain having to inform Maniu personally of the apparent Soviet change of heart.[53] On 22 November, de Chastelain made his first attempt to parachute into Romania. After finding no signals at the dropping zone, the plane turned back but an error in navigation over Albania caused it to run short of fuel and de Chastelain and the crew bailed out off the Italian coast near Brindisi. The place chosen for landing in Romania, an estate called Storobăneasă situated twenty miles north of the Danube and south-east of the town of Alexandria, belonged to the Racotta family. Alexandru (Sandu) Racotta, a staunch anglophile and close friend of Rică Georgescu, had visited Georgescu in prison and on one visit had been asked to help the *Autonomous* mission. Racotta agreed. Racotta and 'Reginald' had been charged by Georgescu with waiting at the dropping zone for de Chastelain, but their car broke down and they were unable to get there.

De Chastelain's second attempt was made with Ivor Porter, a former English-language teacher in Bucharest, recruited into SOE in spring 1941 after leaving Romania. They took off on 5 December, but failed to spot the ground signals giving them the all-clear to jump and returned to Egypt. On the third occasion, they were accompanied by a

---

52 Porter, *Operation Autonomous*, 78.
53 Ibid., 102.

Romanian sabotage expert, Silviu Mețianu.⁵⁴ At 00.30 hours on 22 December the three men were dropped in thick mist. They landed fourteen kilometres from the dropping zone. With whistles to help them locate each other, de Chastelain and Porter soon met up, but it took them over two hours to find Mețianu. They hid in a wood until daybreak and then set out to find the car that should have been awaiting them. De Chastelain asked a peasant woman for directions, but on their way back they were seen by gendarmes and civilians with rifles who fired over their heads. They were escorted to the gendarmerie post in Ploșca, a village some 100 km to the south-west of Bucharest, where they were welcomed by the local dignatories and given a hearty meal. From there they were driven to the police headquarters in Bucharest where they remained until their release on 23 August 1944. Their radio transmitter, code-named *Reginald*, went with them.⁵⁵

Direction-finding equipment told the Germans about the presence of an aircraft near Ploșca and two German soldiers tried to reach the party but were turned away by the local officials. During their internment in Bucharest, Berlin requested on several occasions that de Chastelain be handed over to them but Marshal Antonescu steadfastly refused. Two German officers were allowed to question the group under Romanian supervision. Senior Romanian officials interrogated the group independently, including General C.Z. Vasiliu, deputy minister of the interior, Eugen Cristescu, head of the secret service, and General Constantin Tobescu of the gendarmerie. The prisoners were treated well, were taken for occasional drives, and de Chastelain was allowed to undergo dental treatment in town. At the end of March, Vasiliu, Cristescu and Tobescu visited de Chastelain in turn. They told him of their concern at the Russian advance and their fear for their own and their families' safety.

The Russian advance upon Romania made a deep impression on Churchill. The Prime Minister's position on Russia's western frontiers had changed considerably during the two years since January 1942. Minuting Eden on 16 January 1944 he admitted:

> Undoubtedly my own feelings have changed in the two years that have passed.....The tremendous victories of the Russian armies, the deep-seated changes which have taken place in the character of the Russian State and Government, the new confidence which has grown in our hearts towards Stalin – these have all had

---

54 Silviu Mețianu, born on 23 June 1893 in Făgăraș, was a resident of Barford, England.
55 Porter, *Operation Autonomous*, 111–18.

their effect. Most of all is the fact that the Russians may very soon be in physical possession of these territories, and it is absolutely certain that we should never attempt to turn them out.[56]

Maniu failed to appreciate this change – as did Antonescu. Maniu retained a pre-war image of Britain, coloured by a belief in Britain's imperial might and an assumption that Churchill would contest Soviet ambitions in Eastern Europe. The British did little to disabuse him of his view. When Antonescu was summoned to Germany after the German occupation of Hungary on 19 March 1944, Mihai Antonescu sent a message to the British via Istanbul asking what Allied help Romania could count on. General Wilson, the Commander-in-Chief, Middle East, urged the Marshal not to visit Hitler and to order his troops to cease resistance to the Red Army. Antonescu could count on air support. On 20 March, Wilson had a message from Maniu enquiring what assistance the Allies could give in the event of a *coup*. Wilson said that Romania's future was linked to her determination to overthrow the Antonescu regime and that powerful air attacks would be directed against targets indicated by Maniu, but the sentence "no land assistance can be given from this theatre" was removed by the Foreign Office from his draft, thereby laying the seeds of misunderstanding between Maniu and the western Allies. Within 72 hours Molotov had told the British Ambassador in Moscow that the Soviet government was ready to deal with both Antonescu and Maniu. He suggested that Wilson's reply should be supplemented by another telegram proposing that Antonescu appoint a competent person to liaise between the Soviet and Romanian high commands. This message was transmitted to both Antonescu and Maniu via 'Reginald', and when he received it the Marshal asked for an independent line of communication between himself and Cairo via the Autonomous transmitter held by the gendarmerie.[57]

On 26 March, Vasiliu told de Chastelain that on his return from Germany Antonescu had found General Wilson's telegram and now wished to use the Autonomous cypher and radio to send a reply. The reply was maudlin. "Do not ask an old man and honest soldier to end his days in humility," Antonescu pleaded, addressing Wilson as "a great and glorious soldier" who should not force him to throw his people "into the bottomless pit of shame and destruction. We are your friends not enemies." No country with its forces almost intact "as are ours" could

---

56   Ibid., 92.
57   Ibid., 142.

capitulate "without some serious guarantee of her future."⁵⁸ Transmission of the telegram was delayed. On the evening of 29 March, when de Chastelain and Porter were due to send the reply, they discovered that the crystals of their wireless transmitter were missing – they had been given by Cristescu to the Germans. De Chastelain told Tobescu that SOE had sent Maniu a transmitter in February 1942 and suggested that Maniu be asked to lend this set. On 2 April 1944, de Chastelain was taken to see Maniu. He urged Maniu to carry out a *coup* as soon as possible since the retreat of the Germans in the east made conditions propitious. Maniu informed him that he had disclosed the existence of the 'Reginald' transmitter to the Romanians⁵⁹ – the reason for doing so was not clear – and it was this set that was used to send Antonescu's message.⁶⁰

Antonescu's tolerance and use of the channel with Cairo underlined the significance to the British of the line of communication offered by the SOE presence in Romania. In psychological terms, it provided an enormous boost to active opponents of the Antonescu regime, principally Maniu and the young King Michael, but in political ones it shed no light on the intentions of the Western Allies towards Romania.

---

58 Ibid., 143–44.
59 *23 August 1944. Documente*, vol. II (Bucharest: Editura Ştiinţifică şi Enciclopedică, 1984), 804. King Michael had three W/T sets, two in the attic of the palace, and one in the woods outside Bucharest. Damage to the latter, and the breakdown of the palace sets, prompted de Chastelain to fly to Istanbul on 24 August to obtain military support for Michael's coup. On the following day, Ivor Porter, Ţurcanu (Reginald) and Rică Georgescu found each other and restored wireless communication with Cairo from the vault of the National Bank on one of the palace sets that they had rescued after the German bombing of the palace.
60 Information about the wireless sets sent into Romania clandestinely by SOE was given by Colonel David Talbot Rice in a letter to A. Dew of the Foreign Office dated 1 June 1944: "I did not mention two of the sets which had not been in operation for a very long time. These are both in the possession of Maniu, one having been sent in November 1941 and the other in March 1942... neither of these is in working order. The other sets... are as follows: 1. The set known as REGINALD which has worked on and off until 4.5.44 but which then went off the air and has not come up since; 2. The set taken in by De Chastelain which was captured by the Romanians with him and in March was believed to be in the possession of Marshal Antonescu; 3. The set in possession of Maniu which has so far never worked; 4. The set sent in by a Romanian agent, which has never operated; 5. The set sent in on 27 May of this year addressed to Buzeşti [Grigore Niculescu-Buzeşti, head of the cipher section in the Romanian Foreign Ministry, who was in close contact with King Michael] in the Romanian Foreign Office." The National Archives, FO 371/44000.

The Foreign Office view of Maniu

Maniu did not enjoy enthusiastic favour in parts of the Foreign Office. His indecisiveness in early 1942 and unwillingness to take firm political decisions undermined confidence in him in London after the 23 August *coup*. A minute from a senior Foreign Office official, dated 3 November 1944, stated that "Air Vice Marshal Stevenson [Head of the British Military Mission] was perfectly correct in refusing to see M. Maniu and it is a pity that he did not refuse to see Maniu's intermediary. Maniu seems to be nothing but a drivelling old fool and I can quite sympathise with the Russians if they are trying to get rid of him by fair means or foul."[61]

Maniu was a source of embarassment to Churchill. Maniu's words, reported to London on 1 December 1944, that he would understand it if the British government wanted Romania to cast in her lot with Russia rather than the West, but would be grateful to receive word from them to this effect, stung the Prime Minister into minuting to Eden, "Surely we are not called upon to make such an admission."[62] Maniu begged repeatedly to be told whether Romania had been traded into the Soviet sphere of influence, and each time British representatives were instructed to deny this. Several years later, Archibald Clark Kerr, the British ambassador in Moscow who visited Bucharest in 1945, confessed that one of the most distasteful things he had ever been asked to do was to lie to a man like Maniu.[63] These lies led Maniu, and other democratic leaders in Romania, to compromise themselves unwittingly in the eyes of the Soviets in actions which cost them their liberty and condemned them to spend their final years in prison.

Maniu's attempts to reconcile his pro-Allied sympathies with his contempt for totalitarian rule and mistrust of the Soviet Union gave the British the impression of vacillation and indecision. His refusal to participate in the government appointed by King Michael after the *coup* on 23 August 1944 proved to be a major tactical error because the National Peasant Party was more easily relegated to the sidelines as the Soviet Union imposed its will on Romania. The suppression of the democratic process required the elimination of the 'historical' parties. The arrest of senior figures in the National Peasant Party while trying to flee the country on 14 July 1947 provided the communist-led

---

61 The National Archives, FO 371/44054. Minute dated 3 November 1944, p. 3. I am grateful to Daniel Brett for this reference.
62 Barker, *British Policy*, 242.
63 Porter, *Operation Autonomous*, 238.

government with a pretext for arresting Maniu and his deputy Ion Mihalache on 25 July on the grounds of plotting to overthrow the state.[64] They and several other prominent members of the National Party were tried, found guilty and given life sentences on 11 November. After four years in Galaţi prison (14 November 1947–14 August 1951) Maniu was transferred to Sighet jail where he died on 5 February 1953.[65]

Conclusion

'Shattered illusions' might best describe the sentiments held equally by the British authorities and the Romanian opposition. In the British case, they applied to Maniu's seemingly vacillating opposition to Antonescu; in Maniu's case, his sense of betrayal by the Western Allies. During the war the military situation was never conducive to a defection strategy for Romania, but the fact that the British authorities failed to dispel the illusion cherished by Romanians that there was a chance of surrender to the Western Allies played into the hands of Nazi Germany and their anti-Soviet friends in Romania, and weakened the position of the Romanian opposition.

Upon the conclusion of the war the British and the Americans were faced with a Soviet Union in military occupation of much of Central and Eastern Europe. Their thoughts turned to damage-limitation, but without an effective lever of sanction, apart from the military option which no senior politician in the wake of a long war was prepared to countenance, they were reduced to the role of spectators in the Soviet colonization of the region. Yet in the eyes of many in Eastern Europe, the West had compromised its own principles. By failing to honour the pledge in the Declaration on Liberated Europe, made at the end of the Yalta Conference in February 1945, to "foster the conditions in which the liberated peoples may exercise ... the right of all peoples to choose the form of government under which they will live,"[66] Britain and the United States gave the appearance of legitimacy to what Churchill himself called

---

64   4,600 National Peasant Party members had been arrested four days earlier. Virgiliu Ţârău, "Teroarea pe cote: eliminarea structurilor politice şi ale societăţii civile din România, 1947–1950," presentation given at the International Conference *The Centenary of the October Revolution 1917. 100 Years of Repression*, Sighet, 12–15 October 2017.
65   Andrea Dobeş, *Ilie Lazăr* (Cluj-Napoca: Argonaut, 2006), 176.
66   *The Declaration of Liberated Europe, Yalta Conference, February 1945*, no date, http://highered.mheducation.com/sites/dl/free/0072849037/35264/01_5_liberated_europe.html, accessed 22 October 2017.

"force and misrepresentation."[67] It was this failure which damaged the West most in public opinion in the eastern half of Europe in the postwar period; and in the minds of many of its inhabitants events today in the region conjure up ghosts from that past.

---

67 "The Soviets," Churchill wrote to Roosevelt on 8 March 1945, had established "the rule of a Communist minority by force and misrepresentation." Kevin Ruane, *Churchill and the Bomb in the Cold War* (London: Bloomsbury Academic, 2016), 104.

The Queen Is No Sister: Three Faces of Marie of Romania

Maria Bucur

Abstract: *This essay provides a gender analysis of Queen Marie of Romania's autobiographical works to ask how we can best make sense of this complex and much discussed historical character during World War I as a woman of her time. My focus will be on her work as a politician/diplomat during the war; her efforts on behalf of the military campaign, particularly medical aid and other related services; and her relationship with the feminists who sought to gain the vote during the war. My conclusions offer some appreciative, though overall critical evaluations of the efforts Marie of Romania made in terms of using her dynastic position and popularity on behalf of other women.*

No other woman in Romania's past has seen as much sustained attention as Queen Marie.[1] Charismatic, talented, beautiful, and ambitious, she forcefully redefined the role of the monarchy in Romania throughout World War I and in the interwar period. Some of the historiography dedicated to her life fits in the hagiographic biopic genre, while other writings seem interested in disparaging portrayals, focusing on the alleged licentiousness of her private life.[2] Most of these works speak

---

1   I would like to thank the staff at the Library of the Romanian Academy and the National Military Museum for their assistance with research on this article. I am also grateful for the critiques offered by the anonymous peer reviewers of this article.
2   Adrian Cioroianu and Mihaela Simina, *Maria a României. Regina care a iubit viața și patria* (Bucharest: Curtea Veche, 2015); Alin Ciupală, *Bătălia lor: Femeile din România în primul război mondial* (Iași: Polirom, 2017); Terence Elsberry, *Marie of Romania: The Intimate Life of a Twentieth Century Queen* (New York: St. Martin's Press, 1972); Diana Fotescu and Diana Mandache, *Life of Queen Marie of Romania in Images* (Iași: Center for Romanian Studies, 2003); Guy Gauthier, *Missy. Reine de Roumanie* (Paris: France-empire, 1994); Julia P. Gelardi, *Born to Rule: Fie Reigning Consorts, Granddaughters of Queen Victoria* (New York: St. Martin's Press, 2005); Diana Mandache, *Americans and Queen Marie of* Romania (Iași: Center for Romanian Studies, 1998); Della Marcus, *Her Eternal Crown: Queen Marie of Romania and the Baha'i Faith* (Welwyn, UK: George Ronald Publisher, 2000); Dan Mihăilescu, *Castelul, biblioteca, pușcăria: trei vămi ale feminității exemplare* (Bucharest: Humanitas, 2013); Georges Oudard, *La reine Marie de Roumanie* (Paris: Plon, 1939); Hannah Pakula, *The Last Romantic: A Biography of Queen Marie*

primarily to the authors' understanding of gender norms without much self-reflexivity about their assumptions and provide little interest in actually understanding the historical context Marie lived in from a gender perspective. A recent study on women in Romania during World War I makes a first attempt to understand the documents related to her life during that time in its larger historical context, without much thought given to gender norms at that time.[3] This essay provides a gender analysis of some of her autobiographical works and other relevant texts from the time, to ask how we can best make sense of this complex and much discussed historical character during World War I as a woman of her time.

I focus on her work as a politician/diplomat during the war; her efforts on behalf of the war effort, particularly medical aid and related services; and her relationship with the feminists who sought to gain the vote during and after the war. My conclusions offer some appreciative, though overall critical evaluations of the efforts Marie of Romania made in terms of using her dynastic position and popularity on behalf of other women.

Methods and Assumptions

When someone writes about themselves throughout their adult life, it seems appropriate to use these autobiographical texts to make sense of their values, personality, and self-understanding in whatever capacity they chose to describe themselves.[4] In the case of Queen Marie, we have ample resources.[5] She wrote incessantly and virtually every day. She kept a diary during and after the war. She wrote letters to her mother, sister, and close and distant relations among the European royalty in Britain, Germany, and Russia. She wrote propaganda articles in the Romanian wartime press, often about her own experiences or impressions. She

---

    of Roumania (New York: Simon and Schuster, 1984); Adrian-Silvan Ionescu, *Regina Maria și America* (Bucharest: NOI Media Print, 2009).
3   Ciupală, *Bătălia lor.*
4   Marcin Kafar and Monika Modrzejewska-Świgulska, eds., *Autobiography, Biography, Narration: Research Practice for Biographical Perspectives* (Łódź: Łódź University Press; Kraków: Jagiellonian University Press, 2014).
5   Her autobiographical published works include: *Gânduri și icoane din vremea războiului* (Bucharest: Pavel Suru, 1919); *Însemnări zilnice.* Vol. 1, *Decembrie 1918–Decembrie 1919* (Bucharest: Albatros, 1996); *Însemnări zilnice*, 9 vols. (Bucharest: Historia, 2006); *Ordeal: The Story of My Life*, 2 vols. (New York: C. Scribner's Sons, 1935); *Țara mea* (Bucharest: Pavel Suru, 1919); *The Story of My Life*, 2 vols. (New York: Arno Press, 1971).

wrote an 800-page autobiography that covers her life up to the end of World War I.

Such writings were intended for very different audiences, some private and intimate, like her correspondence with her mother, others strategic and public, like her propaganda articles. These writings offer a rich cross section of her style, recurrent phraseology, favorite themes, questions and issues she was interested in. Marie was careful in crafting her literary persona; the words she put on paper were not an un-edited flow of thoughts, even in her diaries. As she included fragments of her diary from the war in her autobiography, we come to realize that her journal was never penned simply for herself, but had an imagined audience of many and diverse readers. Explanations and details that would be unnecessary if one wrote simply to oneself, to remember exactly what happened or how one felt on a particular day, appear quite often. She was constantly explaining events and one has to wonder: to whom and with what purpose? To her future self, to others? To better understand her own feelings, to sharpen her craft, to find the perfect turn of phrase that could communicate to others the texture of her emotions and impressions from every day?

Other historians have also noted Marie's strategic use of different forms of communication, from word to image and performance, to present her ideas, mobilize support, persuade, charm, and criticize.[6] Therefore, the historical evidence she carefully curated and left behind had that intention in mind. This is why I hesitate to invoke other historical sources from the time, except as additional material that could confirm or challenge certain claims by the queen, as well as provide additional necessary context.

Finally, in terms of the temporal limits of this essay, my focus is primarily on the queen's autobiographical writings about the war. My analysis is provocative, not comprehensive. It calls for a different set of questions and ways of linking various aspects of the queen's public and private personas more closely, from a squarely feminist perspective. How she engaged with the peace-making process at Versailles or with becoming the public face of Romania during her trip to the United States in 1926 would make the subject of a longer and more complex study than afforded in this space.

---

6   Ciupală, *Bătălia lor*.

A Biographical Sketch

Marie was the product of an aristocratic social and cultural milieu that was on its waning days in Europe. She was raised in castles, palaces, and sumptuous villas in Great Britain, Malta, and Germany before marrying Ferdinand and moving to Romania. A relative of many among Europe's royalty, such as Queen Victoria of England, Tsar Nicholas II of Russia and Kaiser Wilhelm of Germany, Marie's familial network provided her with endless forms of support and role models as a young princess. But she did not grow up with a formal education or even a very good informal one, or with much understanding of the world outside the privileged perspective she was born into.[7]

Questions of empowerment or power differences, gender or otherwise, were not part of this universe. Duty and honor to one's family and the aristocratic privilege of her birth informed her upbringing. The person who figured most prominently in her childhood as a moral force was her mother, whose strong sense of moral authority in relation to her children was a recurrent theme in Marie's autobiography. Her father was mostly absent from this universe, a figure of myth and mystery rather than authority and adulation. Though strict in many ways, Marie's mother appears to have allowed her daughter's romantic nature to grow wings early on.

However, when young Marie needed more formal tutoring, her mother's choices were almost invariably traditional and very strict.[8] There is no evidence that her parents or Marie had great interest in intellectual pursuits. That is not to say that Marie did not read widely and was not interested in some prominent thinkers of her time. Nietzsche in particular appears recurrently in her autobiography, connecting to her own romantic notions of fate.[9]

Marie had no knowledge or interest in the feminist rising stars of the late nineteenth century. If she ever read Harriett Taylor or John Stuart Mill, they left no mark on her. By the time of Marie's birth in 1875, Florence Nightingale had become a very famous and much respected figure both among women reformers and the royal family.[10] Her writings

---

7   Marie, Queen of Romania, *Ordeal*, vol. 1.
8   Ibid.
9   Marie, Queen of Romania, *The Story*, vol. 1, p. 586. While recent scholarship has sought feminist interpretations of Nietzsch, most feminist analyses have underscored the misogynistic aspects of his writings. Maudemarie Clark, *Nietzsche on Ethics and Politics* (New York: Oxford University Press, 2015), chapter 7.
10 Mark Bostridge, *Florence Nightingale: The Making of an Icon* (New York: Farrar, Straus, and Giroux, 2008).

on nursing had been printed many times and after her experiences in the Crimean War, she had pleaded in person with Queen Victoria to allow women a more active role in medical training. Marie never mentions Nightingale or her role in modernizing nursing. The work of Millicent Fawcett, whose feminist activities on behalf of women's access to education and political representation were very well publicized in Marie's youth, seemingly left the princess equally cold.[11]

Queen Victoria, her grandmother, was the only other strong female figure in her young years. In her autobiography, Marie underscored important elements of Victoria's personality that provide clues for understanding the princess's views on gender norms among European royalty. She depicted Victoria as restrained in her show of power, with an element of quirkiness that puzzled and endeared her to the young granddaughter.[12] Fair and generous in the interactions Marie observed, the queen appeared like a model of responsible and loveable authority.

Other female figures of sustained interest in Marie's writings were her sister Victoria, affectionately known as "Ducky," and Queen Elisabeth of Romania.[13] Marie and Ducky were a year apart and inseparable in their childhood. According to Marie, "Ducky usually played the heroic, brave, self-sacrificing parts, and was almost always a male. There was something heroic about Ducky, ...something a little somber. She was the one who espoused causes, ...who allowed no nonsense.... She was strong and rebellious."[14] In this autobiography written when the queen was in her fifties, the earliest mention of gender norms is this passage dedicated to her sister. As an aging woman, Marie saw her sister as the yin to her yang, complementary and opposite in many ways. Her words suggest how the queen saw herself in relation to gender norms, not just her sister. To look at any images of Victoria, the description "almost male" never comes to mind. It is clearly in relation to behavior and very much in contrast to femininity that she defines Ducky's role-playing. Marie's description also implies that she generally did not favor playing the same role, preferring to be the girl, the more feminine one in their games. The passage provides clues as to what "playing the male" meant, and by extension, in Marie's

---

11   Fawcett was a middle-of-the-road reformist leader in the movement by comparison with Emmeline Pankhurst, which why I single out Fawcett as a name Marie might have heard about. June Purvis, *Emmeline Pankhurst: A Biography* (London: Routledge, 2002).
12   Marie, Queen of Romania, *Ordeal*, vol. 1.
13   These are not the only women about whom Marie wrote on repeated occasions, but for the purposes of this short study, I focus on these important formative figures.
14   Marie, Queen of Romania, *The Story*, vol. 1, p. 64.

polarized view of gender roles, how it differed from "playing the female." She listed heroism, bravery, self-sacrifice, strength, rebelliousness, and espousing causes as core elements of Ducky's behavior, and acknowledged she admired them, without wanting to imitate this behavior.

This description of Marie's own distance from such "male" behavior appears more puzzling in view of subsequent references in her autobiography, journal and other writings to herself as rebellious, espousing causes (of Greater Romania in particular), and head-strong during the war. At other points, she made mention of other people's view of her as brave and heroic. It seems the queen was at odds with her own polarized view of gender norms: the war had pushed Marie far outside of her comfort zone in this regard, without forcing her to question these norms.

Another prominent female figure at the opposite pole of Marie's unrestrained admiration for her sister was Queen Elisabeth of Romania, on the throne when Marie arrived in Bucharest as a bride of seventeen. Marie described Elisabeth as mercurial and driven by her sense of drama and romantic musings, rather than rational thought. Elisabeth had produced no male heirs for the crown and replaced motherhood with a salon of artists, musicians, and writers as the focus of her passions and source of some authority in Romanian society. Elisabeth herself was a writer and somewhat of an artist, though Marie clearly thought very little of her aunt's artistic talents.[15]

The autobiography moves from wanting to render Marie's negative first impressions of the queen to providing an appreciative portrait at the end of Elisabeth's life. Despite this stated intention, the description of Elisabeth is condescending:

> Nothing was ever taken calmly, everything had to be rapturous, tragic, excessive or extravagantly comic. Aunty always imagined she was discovering rare souls. She could not admit those around her to be ordinary.... In later years I understood Aunty better and her hungry longing for what had been denied her, that aching longing which turned to envy when I, little realizing what I represented, invaded her darkened sanctuary with my insolent youth.[16]

A daily presence in Marie's life between 1893 and 1916, when she passed away, Elisabeth became an example of how *not* to wield power as a queen and restrain feminine irrational instincts that Marie assumed were a natural part of Elisabeth's personality. Watching Elisabeth's interactions

---

15 Marie, Queen of Romania, *Ordeal*, vol. 1., especially chapter 11.
16 Marie, Queen of Romania, *The Story*, vol. 1, 348.

with King Carol I, her entourage, and high society became lessons for Marie in how not to behave as a woman and a monarch.

Was Marie unusual among women of her social standing in her upbringing, values, and views about power, responsibility, and gender roles? There isn't much evidence to suggest she was. Unique in her case is the particularity that Romania presents in the history of monarchical regimes in Europe, along with the other newly-established Balkan states. The foreign-born princes and princesses, kings and queens who came to sit on the throne in Romania, Bulgaria, Serbia, Greece, and Albania, represented a compromise orchestrated by the monarchical regimes of the European Great Powers. Their hope was that these rulers would bring the imprimatur of their aristocratic values to the overwhelmingly peasant societies they were to lead. But these were societies that, by the beginning of the twentieth century, had developed their own dynamic engagement with modernization, inclusive of movements for women's empowerment in education, civil rights, and even suffrage.

The lack of a long history of dynastic rule together with these developments from below allowed for a more diverse engagement on the part of female royals with challenges to the established patriarchal norms and institutions than in countries where the role of those female royals had long been formally defined. In this regard, the contrast between the roles of Queen Marie in Romania and Queen Eleonora in Bulgaria is instructive. It shows the extent to which each made specific choices about what to become, and what path not to take as a powerful symbol and agent at the top of their countries' social hierarchy. Eleonora focused most of her public activism on developing and supporting opportunities for women in education, such as nursing and access to higher education, and entrepreneurship, such as lacemaking.[17] Marie did not.

The Politician

King Carol I passed away at the beginning of World War I on 10 October 1914, before making any decision regarding Romania's participation in the war. He left the political leadership divided in their loyalties towards the Central Powers versus the Entente. Marie was a close relation to royalty on both sides of the conflict, and thus embattled in her evolving sentiments. But she quickly became a resolute and outspoken supporter of the Entente.

---

17 Vladimir Tsanoff, "Queen Eleanora's Visit," *Harper's* Weekly 58, 30 May 1914, 18–9.

In her autobiography, the queen wrote somewhat disingenuously: "I was...almost reprehensibly indifferent to politics, even to those of my country, having, because of Uncle's [Carol I] complete absorption in them, a horror even of the word 'politics'."[18] She continued by stating that she simply wanted to be loved by her people, her "chief urge was towards independence and a mighty desire to live my life as agreeably as possible, but in my own way." She claimed that politics was a game over power and control over others, and that she wished none of that for herself.

Yet Marie spent most of her waking hours between 1914 and 1919 writing letters to foreign potentates on behalf of Romania's interests, meeting with prime ministers, Romanian generals, and representatives of foreign governments to persuade them about specific actions in the war, and writing propaganda pieces on behalf of the war effort in the Romanian press. Both her writings and the personal accounts by some of Romania's most prominent politicians during that period confirm the queen's direct engagement in the internal and external affairs of the country in direct contraction to her own statements later on.[19] Some viewed her persistency as undue influence, in line with the mainstream views of the monarchy's role and gender norms.[20] While Elisabeth had remained active strictly in the areas of charity and the arts, both considered appropriate for a Queen, Marie insisted on having a very public opinion about Romania's alliances with the Great Powers and on Romanian irredentism. As one can garner from Marie's discussion of her predecessor, she wanted to be nothing like Elisabeth, and, once the old queen passed away, Marie proceeded to craft her own role with little regard for precedent.

One might view this independent streak as acting out against established gender roles, but there is little evidence of such rebelliousness. As a princess, Marie saw her privileged position and power as a natural given. At most, she used her beauty and feminine charisma as a tool for the very political goals she wished to accomplish, above all Romania's irredentist aspirations in Transylvania.

The actions of the queen need to be understood also in terms of the unprecedented nature of the war and the specific complexities of Romania's predicament at that time. Elisabeth had been queen during two important wars for Romania's status as a new kingdom in the Balkans, the

---

18 Ibid., 559.
19 Alexandru Averescu, *Notițe zilnice de război*, 2 vols. (Bucharest: Institutul de Arte Grafice and Editura Apollo, 1937); Ioan G. Duca, *Memorii*, Vol. 4, *Războiul, partea a II-a (1917–1919)* (Bucharest: Editura Machiavelli, 1994).
20 Ciupală, *Bătălia lor*.

Russo-Turkish War of 1877–78 and the Second Balkan War (1913), but neither was fought on Romanian soil, and therefore involved little direct interaction with the civilian population.[21] Neither was lengthy in duration in terms of Romania's own participation. Though casualties were somewhat high, they were limited to men in uniform.[22] The male political and military leadership at that time did not see the queen playing any role in relation to the war effort, except encouraging volunteer nursing efforts strictly in relation to epidemics, not battlefield casualties. Initially Queen Marie expressed interest in playing a direct public role by assisting with the cholera epidemic outbreak during the Second Balkan War that killed 6,000 soldiers.

World War I was different from any previous military conflict.[23] The Great Powers had become irreconcilably divided, with old alliances, such as Russia's with the Habsburg Empire now tossed aside in favor of joining forces with Britain and France against the Germans. Romania had irredentist aspirations in Transylvania (controlled by the Habsburgs), Bessarabia (controlled by the Russians) and Dobrogea (controlled by the Bulgarians) and therefore no obvious path forward in terms of either self-interest or established loyalties of the political leadership. King Ferdinand could have been the decisive voice in this deadlock. But he wasn't.

There is evidence in both Marie's writings and those of others from the time that the queen decided to act publicly out of frustration with her husband's indecisive personality. [24] Her journal and autobiography contain multiple statements about her desperation at his chronic indecision: "If Nando [King Ferdinand] would be left alone, nothing would get done—what world does he live in? What sort of head does he have on his shoulders? What heart?" [25] Marie was trapped in a paradoxical situation. She had married a man who understood his military and political royal duties as exclusively his and viewed his wife's role primarily in terms of raising the royal offspring and supporting him. Her upbringing directed Marie towards upholding this secondary role. Yet her ambitions ran much higher: she wanted to be loved and command the loyalty of her subjects by performing a much larger role as partner to the

---

21 Keith Hitchins, *Rumania: 1866–1947* (Oxford: Clarendon Press, 1994).
22 Romania lost 10,000 troops in the 1877 War of Independence.
23 For the most comprehensive historical analysis of the war, see Constantin Kirițescu, *Istoria războiului pentru întregirea României: 1916–1919* (Bucharest: Editura Casei Școalelor, 1922–3).
24 Ciupală, *Bătălia lor*.
25 Marie, Queen of Romania, *Jurnal de război, 1916–1917* (Bucharest: Humanitas, 2014), 170.

king, helping him come to the important decisions he seemed unable to reach on his own.

On 14 January 1917, she stated: "What makes my work so difficult and often makes me feel so helpless is that I have no actual power in my hands, only the right to try and help, to give ideas, to persuade, to try and unify action; but an actual recognized *right* to order about, I have not."[26] When Marie wrote about her lack of power, was she naïve, disingenuous, or was she expressing something else? It seems her frustration rested in not having any formal authority as the consort of the king, her role resting entirely in the realm of persuasion and charm. She never went so far as to connect this frustration to the larger structural issue of how gender regimes shaped expectations about the lives of women even among the most privileged royalty.

On the contrary, Marie repeatedly invoked her gender identity in natural, essentialist terms, rather than as a socially constructed liability: "my appreciations [about politics] could easily be considered too feminine, too biased"[27]; "Ferdinand was the kindest of souls and was always ready to listen to [my] feminine pleadings[28]; "woman-like I jumped to conclusions."[29] On a single occasion did Marie express a critical view of gender norms: "I know many things which I cannot talk about. Sometimes it is desperate to be a woman, for a woman is not supposed to be able to help, and yet sometimes she can see a situation with painful clearness!"[30] Writing two months after Romania's entry in the war, when poor planning and internal dissent among politicians and the military were leading to mounting casualties, Marie expressed her frustration with the established order in more clearly gendered terms than before. She saw herself as a wasted resource for the war effort, and recognized that this desperate situation was due to gender norms of the time, including those of her husband, that women had no business in politics and military planning.

As the war continued, Marie used her "painful clearness" through surrogates, such as her son, Carol II: "Carol gave my message [to the Crown Council] bravely, and when he came back he fell on my neck, thanking me for having allowed him, through my words, to express his

---

26   Marie, Queen of Romania, *The Story*, vol. 2, p. 120, italics in the original.
27   Marie, Queen of Romania, *The Story*, vol. 1, p. 409.
28   Marie, Queen of Romania, *The Story*, vol. 2, p. 4.
29   Ibid., 5.
30   Ibid., 82.

own feelings."[31] Others whom the king trusted, such as Barbu Stirbey, also conveyed some of her concerns.[32]

Marie wrote her foreign relatives, including Tsar Nicholas II and King George V, to continue their support for Romania's military operations and political aspirations after 1916.[33] While some of these letters may have been a result of requests by Ferdinand, more often they were at the queen's initiative. Finally, as the war proceeded, many politicians and military leaders figured out that Marie was an important informal advisor to the king and the person most likely to persuade him into action, among them Ion Brătianu, gen. Alexandru Averescu, gen. Eremia Grigorescu, and gen. Henri Berthelot. The number of prominent men who requested meetings with the queen and sought to influence her views about the course of the war grew steadily, a statement to her growing informal power as the king's confidante.[34]

Though not always successful, Marie was persistent on issues she dearly cared about, such as keeping Romania in the war and securing Transylvania after the war. Her pragmatism in methods matched her passion when it came to personal convictions, and Marie made no apologies in writing during and after the war about the choices she made. She saw herself fully vindicated after the war and believed she had earned her place at the head of the triumphal return to Bucharest, riding proudly next to her husband.[35]

---

31 Ibid., 314.
32 Ciupală, *Bătălia lor*.
33 Marie, Queen of Romania, *The Story*, vol. 2.
34 Ciupală, *Bătălia lor*, 194.
35 Marie, Queen of Romania, *The Story*, vol. 2, pp. 414–5.

Illustration 1: Mural from the Romanian Atheneum representing King Ferdinand and Queen Marie arriving in Alba Iulia for their coronation of Greater Romania. Photo by Maria Bucur.

The "Mother of the Wounded"

Marie played a direct public role in the war effort in medical and civilian assistance. Today she is known as "the mother of the wounded," a mythological moniker that both reveals and hides important historical facts.[36] Here I present a critical appreciation, inclusive of my own previous depictions, of the queen's medical and charitable contributions to the war effort.

As with the military in general, the state of medical assistance was woefully inadequate in August 1916. Though she talked at length about the 1913 cholera epidemic as having changed her thinking about her role as Queen, Marie did nothing until the summer of 1916 to enhance the preparedness of the medical assistance service for the front. True, she had no official role to play in that regard. But other similarly powerless queens, such as Eleonora of Bulgaria, had taken the epidemic disasters of the Balkan Wars as a clarion call for seriously rethinking the professionalization of nursing in her country.[37] In 1914, Eleonora invited

---

36 For an analysis of the role played by Marie in the war and afterwards, in relation to women's struggle for voting rights, see Maria Bucur, "Between the Mother of the Wounded and the Virgin from Jiu: Romanian Women and the Gender of Heroism during the Great War," *Journal of Women's History* 12, no. 2 (2000): 30-56.

37 Maria Bucur, "Sworn Virgins and Mothers of the Wounded: Balkan Women and World War I," in *Cutting a New Pattern: Uniformed Women in the Great War*, eds.

to Bulgaria an American Red Cross official with experience in nursing training, to help establish a school for nursing. Her efforts were short-lived because of Bulgaria's entry in the war on the side of the Central Powers. But Eleonora continued these activities until her death in 1917, serving actively as a nurse in the war effort.

By contrast, there is no evidence that, after observing the cholera epidemic in 1913, Marie undertook any immediate activities to enhance the training of female nurses to better assist the military. The first state-certified nursing school opened in Bucharest in 1913 at the initiative of Mina Minovici, under the leadership of Hermina Walch-Kaminski, the first woman to complete medical training in Romania.[38] The school had graduated 100 nurses by 1916. Though it subsequently took the name of Queen Marie, there is no evidence that the queen worked with Minovici or Walch-Kaminski on this issue.[39] This contrasts to the frequent mentions Marie made of other medical initiatives, either foreign (Red Cross) or local, especially after the retreat from Bucharest in December 1916, when the Central Powers occupied southern Romania.

When the war's destruction became apparent, as new weaponry produced more extensive and complicated wounds and the widespread unsanitary conditions created foci for epidemics, the queen became concerned: "I am desperate not to be able to help; I feel I ought to be doing something, something useful, something energetic. But what can a woman do in modern war?"[40] There were ample examples of what women had done, from Florence Nightingale during the Crimean War to the indomitable Flora Sandes and relentless Elsie Inglis, both British women who served on the front respectively as officer and doctor in the Balkan Wars and then returned there during World War I.

    Barton C. Hacker and Margaret Vining (Washington, D.C.: Smithsonian Institution Scholarly Press, forthcoming).
38 George Marcu, ed., *Dicționarul personalităților feminine din România* (Bucharest: Editura Meronia, 2009).
39 Ministère de la santé publique, du travail, et de l'assistance sociale, *Exposé general de l'état sanitaire de la Roumanie* (Bucharest: Cartea medicală, 1923).
40 Marie, Queen of Romania, *The Story*, vol. 2, p. 56, entry from 5 September 1916.

Illustration 2: Photograph taken at the nursing school renamed Queen Marie after 1916, with the queen at the center of the group. From Ministère de la santé publique, du travail, et de l'assistance sociale, *Exposé general de l'état sanitaire de la Roumanie* (Bucharest: Cartea medicală, 1923).

To her credit, Marie threw herself into the work of fundraising and persuading able individuals to participate in the war effort with tireless passion. The Cotroceni royal residence in Bucharest was retrofitted into a hospital soon after the war started. Due to aerial bombing of the capital, the royal family had to move to a nearby location in Buftea, on the estate of Barbu Stirbey. The queen started visiting the wounded in the newly established hospital and bringing supplies to them; her personal warmth and charisma were much appreciated by the soldiers.

Marie started working with the Red Cross early on during the war. But she was neither qualified nor did she ever work as a nurse, despite claims to the contrary. Most of the images from the war show her in a white Red Cross outfit, often accompanied by the description "the mother of the wounded." This image served two important purposes. First, postcards and posters with the queen posing as a nurse were sold at fundraising events in Romania and overseas. They helped popularize the cause of Romania abroad, associating Romania with the extremely attractive and irresistibly charming Marie. The queen carefully curated this aspect, together with a staff that included photographers, printers, and even filmmakers.⁴¹

Illustration 3: Front page of *The Daily* Mirror from 24 October 1916, provided by Marie's public relations service as propaganda for the queen's sanitary work.

Secondly, the queen provided a model for many other women who wished to help the war effort. By 1916 a rich variety of women's organizations had begun to develop in Romania, most of them initiated by women of the upper and middle-classes. Many had a narrowly charitable profile, while others focused on enhancing educational and employment opportunities for girls, as well as political and civil rights issues.⁴² When the war started,

---

41 Ciupală, *Bătălia lor*.
42 On the activities of Romanian feminists during that period, as reflected in publications of the period, see Ștefania Mihăilescu, *Emanciparea femeii române: Antologie de texte*. Vol. 1, *1815–1918* (Bucharest: Editura Ecumenică, 2001). For analyses of women's activism during that period, see Maria Bucur, "Between Liberal and Republican Citizenship. Feminism and Nationalism in Romania, 1859– 1918," *Aspasia* 1 (2007): 84–103; Roxana Cheșchebec, "Toward a Romanian

many of these organizations shifted their focus to assisting the war effort by providing food, shelter, and medical help to the military and displaced civilian population. Many other women, left alone as caretakers of their homes for the first time by their husbands, fathers, and sons, were anxiously wishing they could do something useful in this period of crisis.[43]

By visiting hospitals all over Moldavia[44] almost daily, Marie made herself accessible to the wounded, the medical personnel assisting them, and the volunteering civilians, primarily women, who came to help without much training or knowledge about what was needed. Aristocratic women, some of them part of the queen's inner circle, and others wishing to gain access to the queen, followed her lead and offered their money, residences, and time. One princely residence at Coțofănești was turned into a hospital.[45] Other large homes became soup kitchens for the civilian poor or asylums for recovering soldiers who were unable to return home after they were discharged from hospitals.

What the queen could not model was actual expertise in medical matters. She brought flowers, smiles, cigarettes, and other small gifts to the wounded she visited, offering primarily moral support. Such support was no substitute for actual medical help, and some doctors complained about the overcrowding of hospital salons with the many women who wished to follow in Marie's footsteps.[46] Volunteers willing to wash and dress wounds, as well as clean dirty laundry and floors, were in much greater demand than smiles. Thus, while generous and in many ways helpful, some of these performances of love and care had a less desirable and helpful underside, which the queen never commented on, though it is quite likely she heard about these criticisms along the way.

Marie contributed more effectively through financial and personal means. She wrote to her relatives in Russia to request sanitary trains and medical supplies, and received some support in response. The Russians also offered logistical support for the Red Cross volunteers and medical supplies that came from France, Great Britain and the United States, in part at the insistence of the queen. Before February 1917 there was, of

---

Women's Movement. An Organizational History (1880s–1940)," in *Women's Movements: Networks and Debates in Post-Communist Countries in the 19th and 20th Centuries*, eds. Edith Saurer, Margareth Lanzinger, and Elisabeth Frysak (Köln: Böhlau, 2006), 439–55; Paraschiva Câncea, *Mișcarea pentru emanciparea femeii în România 1848–1948* (Bucharest: Editura Politică, 1976).
43 For more on this, see Bucur, "Sworn Virgins," and Ciupală, *Bătălia lor*.
44 This was the part of Romania that remained under the control of the Monarchy between December 1916 and March 1918.
45 Marie, Queen of Romania, *The Story*, vol. 2.
46 Ciupală, *Bătălia lor*.

course, self-interest on the part of the tsarist troops to support the Romanian front, inclusive of medical aid. Afterwards, as the Empire was slowly imploding, the insistence of the queen played a more important role.[47]

She also lent her name and reputation to an ambulance service that helped bring wounded troops to military hospitals. The funds for this ambulance service came from the queen's fundraising efforts, with a manager appointed by Marie herself. The manager was Jean Chrissoveloni, a man with no medical training but with managerial skills, as he was one of the prominent bankers of the day. The queen praised his abilities in her wartime journal and autobiography: "I had a cruel struggle about my 'Regina Maria' ambulances, a well run organization, under my special guidance and of which Jean Chrissoveloni was a leading spirit. We did astonishingly good work, being always there when the need was greatest."[48] There is little verifiable evidence about her skills of providing efficient leadership for the limited human and financial resources available for the ambulance service or the "astonishingly good work" done "when the need was greatest." Finally, it is not clear what "special guidance" the queen provided, given her lack of medical training.

A study of the Romanian medical institutions published in 1923 under the auspices of the government sanitary services makes no mention of Chrissoveloni or the ambulance service he led.[49] As director of the government sanitary services during the war and a frequent visitor to the queen, Cantacuzino provided reports about the state of the war medical support. In her autobiography the queen stated: "I had to have Dr. Jean Cantacuzene named as supreme head of our sanitary organization, which was in a chaotic condition, and black typhus was spreading appallingly."[50] Cantacuzino had been the head of the sanitary services starting in 1908 and made the most important contributions to preparing the army's medical support ahead of the conflict.[51] It is unlikely that he needed the queen's support to take on the job he already held for almost a decade and for which he was the most qualified individual.

---

47 Ibid.
48 Marie, Queen of Romania, *The Story*, vol. 2, p. 127.
49 Ministère de la santé publique, du travail, et de l'assistance sociale, *Exposé general*.
50 Marie, Queen of Romania, *The Story*, vol. 2, p. 127.
51 V. Brădățeanu, "Documentar: Institutul de seruri și vaccinuri „Dr. Ioan Cantacuzino" – sau despre cum ne distrugem institutele de succes," 1 April 2017, http://www.rador.ro/2017/04/01/documentar-institutul-de-seruri-si-vaccinuri-dr-ioan-cantacuzino-sau-despre-cum-ne-distrugem-institutele-de-succes/, accessed 23 August 2018.

Therefore, we need to take the queen's statements about her leadership in organizing the medical services during the war with a grain of salt.

There is no question that Marie's actions and popularity encouraged many women to participate in the war effort. Several journals mention her presence among the Red Cross hospitals as a motivating factor.[52] One autobiography describes how the queen beckoned Jeana Fodoreanu, a trained doctor and the daughter of one of the prominent officers in the medical services, to manage one of the sanitary trains Marie secured for the front.[53] It is possible that Marie herself provided just the right encouragement. Or maybe it was the destruction of the war, the fact that the husbands, sons, and brothers of so many women had been called to arms and left behind desperation and fear. All over Europe, women became involved in the war effort because they needed to survive, and because they could not live with themselves if they did not try to help in some way, as casualties mounted. Some even volunteered as soldiers, including in Romania. As much as Marie relished being called "the mother of the wounded," she was not the only woman in Romania whom others referred to thusly. Elisabeth had been referred to in the same way in 1877, and other women who managed military hospitals in World War I, such as Olga Demetriade, were also referred to as "mothers of the wounded."[54]

In short, though more visible and certainly acting self-consciously as a model, Queen Marie was one among many women in Romania who volunteered for the war effort as best as she could, given the restrictions and inadequacies of Romania's policies regarding women's education and professional development. Though they were encouraged to volunteer, the medical establishment and Romanian Red Cross spared few resources to train women adequately, to hire them and provide these women with the opportunity to serve and the financial tools to survive. In 1923, the amount of money spent on training female nurses, midwives, and male surgical aids was 1.4 million lei, out of 200.3 million lei allocated for medical education overall.[55] A nurse's salary was 300 lei/month, while the driver of the general director made 750 lei/month.[56] During the war, women asked the queen to consider providing voluntary nurses with

---

52 Nelli Cornea, *Insemnări din vremea războiului* (Bucharest: Ed. Librăriei H. Steinberg și fiu, 1921), 28.
53 Jean Col. Fodoreanu, *Femee-Soldat* (Oradea: Tip. Adolf Sonnenfeld S.A., 1928).
54 Cornea, *Insemnări din vremea războiului*, 65.
55 Ministère de la santé publique, du travail, et de l'assistance sociale, Exposé *general*, 118.
56 Ibid., 121.

stipends that would help them offset the rising cost of food and fuel during the war.⁵⁷

The queen did not ponder this issue very much, as there are no references to this problem in her wartime journal. Red Cross personnel from other countries, who are also referred to as volunteers, received a monthly stipend for their expenses and efforts. This was perhaps a reasonable expectation when serving in a foreign country's war effort. But men serving on the front as soldiers, medical aides, or even volunteers received a monthly stipend to make up for some of the income a family lost when the breadwinner was taken into the army. (The funds would not be made automatically available to the wife left behind).⁵⁸ For women who had to assume the role of head of family in terms of securing food, shelter, and other necessities for their families, volunteering for the war effort also meant having fewer hours in the day to take care of their household responsibilities. Receiving a stipend for their efforts seemed both necessary and fundamentally fair, if seen through the lens of the individual effort, rather than any preconception about gender and economic autonomy.⁵⁹ Although she was aware of these issues, the queen offered very little support aside from her own tenacious activities in the hospitals and a medal for these volunteers' service.

Marie and Feminism

As the wife of the Romanian king at a time when feminism was becoming a vibrant movement and women showed a growing interested in challenging educational, property, and professional structural gender inequalities, Marie was a potential lightening rod for these aspirations. Nonetheless, women's legal status saw no improvement with the 1923 Constitution; educational opportunities for women were enhanced through other people's efforts; and feminist lawyers, doctors, architects, and other professional women fought for the right to practice in these fields with no support from the queen.⁶⁰

---

57 Ciupală, *Bătălia lor*, 105.
58 Maria Bucur, "The Economics of Citizenship: Gender Regimes and Property Rights in Romania in the 20th Century," in *Gender and Citizenship in Historical and Transnational Perspective*, eds. Anne Epstein and Rachel Fuchs (Basingstoke: Palgrave, 2016), 143–65.
59 Ibid.
60 There were many well-publicized debates about women's suffrage around the new Constitution, from law journals to political parties. The variety of positions articulated in a public forum is best exemplified by the Atheneum talks hosted by

Marie was not entirely sheltered from the systemic gender inequalities of the day. She experienced misogyny repeatedly in her lifetime, on the part of both the male political and military leadership, as well as women at the court. Though she bemoaned these attitudes on occasion, Marie generally observed them with little critical distance. When told that riding a horse would prevent her from being fertile, she only commented that she found this attitude "queer."[61] It is unlikely she did not see that such ideas were connected to sexist views about women as physically weak. And it is unlikely that her entourage and Romanian tutors did not explain the prevailing negative views of women horseback riders as foreign, unnatural, and therefore out of place with Romanian gender and social norms, as exemplified by Vasile Alecsandri's well-known satirical literary character, Chirița. [62] Through action, Marie challenged these notions every day, eventually prevailed over her critics, and enjoyed the privilege of riding whenever and wherever she wished. But she did so only for herself and her family.

When it came to connecting her own frustrations as a woman with any larger legal, cultural, and economic gender regimes, Marie fell short of fully articulating any feminist critique. In her journal and autobiography, she mentioned feminism only twice. First, in describing the friends who surrounded her at the court as a young princess, she mentioned in passing "Vidine Palady, who had so much to say on every subject and to-day is the principal leader of our feministic movement."[63] Palady was Alexandrina Cantacuzino, who before the war had already become active in the leadership of the National Orthodox Society of Romanian Women.[64] Cantacuzino was outspoken on the issue of women's suffrage, which she framed in religious and nationalistically conservative language. In short, she was not a radical. Marie called Cantacuzino's movement "feministic," a seldom used term. Romanian feminists never used it to refer to themselves and the movement overall. One English-language critic used the term in 1902 to describe Heinrik Ibsen's plays as

---

the Romanian Social Institute. Institutul Social Român, *Constituția din 1923 în dezbaterile contemporanilor* (Bucharest: Humanitas, 1999).
61 Marie, Queen of Romania, *The Story*, vol. 1, p. 360.
62 Vasile Alecsandri, *Chirița în provinție: comedii și cânticele comice* (Bucharest: Corint, 2002).
63 Marie, Queen of Romania, *The Story*, vol. 1, p. 446.
64 Roxana Cheșchebec, "Feminist Ideologies and Activism in Romania (approx. 1890–1940s). Nationalism and Internationalism in Romanian Projects for Women's Emancipation," PhD Diss., Central European University, 2005.

"feministic propaganda." [65] So, what to make of this reference in the queen's autobiography? It is fair to assume she was not close with Cantacuzino, as she only mentioned the feminist leader in passing. Though her words suggest appreciation for Cantacuzino's strong personality (she "had so much to say on every subject"), there is no warmth or intimacy in the description, by contrast with portraits of other women from her entourage, such as Maruka Cantacuzino.

The second reference to feminism in Marie's autobiography comes from her wartime journal, and it is also about Alexandrina Cantacuzino. In describing the hosts of the royal family after having to evacuate the Cotroceni royal palace at the beginning of the hostilities, Marie mentioned "Alexandrine Cantacuzene's place, Ciocănești [sic!]. She was a Paladi by birth, one of the friends of my youth. Small, animated, 'le verbe facil,' [easy with words] she was always earnest and is to-day our foremost feminine leader whose name is well-known through all the reforming world."[66] This portrait is more extensive and generous by comparison with the earlier description of Cantacuzino. To the journal entry, the queen subsequently added the characterization of Cantacuzino as "our foremost feminine leader whose name is well-known through all the reforming world."

This is the closest Marie came to showing earnest admiration for the work of Cantacuzino on behalf of the feminist movement. Indeed, by the early 1930s, when Marie's autobiography was written, Cantacuzino had become active in international networks such as the International Women's Suffrage Alliance, the International Council of Women, and International Alliance of Women, and the League of Nations, and had helped found the Women's Little Entente in 1923.[67] But was Cantacuzino Romania's "foremost feminine leader"? Cantacuzino herself thought so, but others did not agree.

At the end of the war Romania had well over a hundred women's organizations, their ranks greatly enhanced after 1918 by dozens of organizations from Transylvania. In a 1929 memorandum to the Romanian political leadership, Romanian feminists made a renewed bid for gaining the vote, having failed to secure enough support for female suffrage in 1917, 1918, 1919, and 1923. The document was signed by 12

---

65 Margaret Ferguson, "Feminism in Time," *Modern Language* Quarterly, 65, no. 1 (March 2004): 7–8.
66 Marie, Queen of Romania, *The Story*, vol. 2, p. 43.
67 Cheșchebec, "Toward a Romanian Women's Movement," 450.

female leaders on behalf of 150 women's organizations.[68] Alexandrina Cantacuzino was a co-signer, as co-chair of the National Council of Romanian Women, together with Calypso Botez.[69]

The aspirations of these organizations after 1919 were shaped by the experiences of women during the war. Twice during the war, women's suffrage supporters had asked Parliament to give women the vote on the basis of the work they were doing for their country and the contributions they wished to make as full citizens to the nationalist aspirations of the government. Twice they were turned down, but the queen never mentioned this issue.

Bread riots led by women had taken place in Bucharest and other locations during the war, signaling the broader dissatisfaction of the female population with the unbearable situation they were facing in the wartime. When over a million men were recruited into the army (15 percent of the country's total population), their families were left to fend for themselves.[70] These men also represented the main waged labor force and breadwinners in their families, which represented 63 percent or more of the total population of Romania. In short, a majority of the female population of Romania experienced the war as a period of serious economic privation; of resourceful improvisation, inclusive of working for the occupation troops in southern Romania; of humiliating dependence on those 37 percent of the population that were wealthier; and of trying to participate in the war effort as best as these crippling limitations allowed.

Were these issues known to the queen? She prided herself on walking among her people and having their loyalty. In her journal and autobiography, she described visits to soup kitchens and stays in villages with simple peasant women. But she never reflected directly on the gendered aspects of these women's poverty, vulnerability, fears, or ability to prevail over their context of disempowerment and lack of appreciation on the part of male-controlled institutions, from the Red Cross to the military and government. It may be that none of these women ever mentioned their hardships to Marie, but, as I demonstrate, we know that

---

68 As located at the library of the Romanian Academy bound together with Alexandrina Cantacuzino, *Femeile în fața dreptului de vot, programul de luptă al grupuplui femeilor române: Cuvântare, 10 aprilie 1929* (Bucharest: Tipografia Capitalei, 1929).

69 Botez was nowhere mentioned by Queen Marie, and there is no mystery why. She was not part of the Romanian aristocracy, and would not have had access to the Queen as part of her entourage at the court.

70 Bucur, "The Economics of Citizenship."

at least recipients of the Queen Marie Cross described their economic hardships to the queen when they requested financial support for their work as medical volunteers. We also know from private diaries and memoirs of women from that period, that some of them mentioned their frustrations and desperation to members of the aristocracy with access to the queen.[71]

Most directly, a group of feminist activists from the Association for the Civil and Political Emancipation of Romanian Women, including Calypso Botez and Alexandrina Cantacuzino, pleaded with Marie on 18 July 1919 to support their cause for women's enfranchisement on the basis of their war-time contributions. According to Botez and an account published in *Acțiunea Feministă* soon after the audience, Marie "declared she was a partisan in the struggle for women's voting rights and warmly embraced the women's movement in Romania for emancipation."[72] If so, what came of it? There is no evidence that the queen's promises went beyond these conversations. She took no public stance on the matter in 1917 and 1918, when she was in Iași, while feminist leaders were publicly articulating reasons why women deserved and the country needed them to become full citizens, with voting rights, access to all education and professional opportunities, and the same civil rights (property, inheritance) as men.[73]

The most Marie offered as public support for women's activities in the wartime was the Queen Marie Cross, which she helped found on 17 March 1917 for "ladies and gentlemen who distinguish themselves on sanitary matters."[74] The king rather than queen officially awarded this decoration, but Marie played an active role in establishing the decoration and identifying many of the candidates, especially among women. By the end of the war, 3,109 Queen Marie Crosses had been awarded, 1,264 of them to women.[75] Some of these decorations went to British, Russian, French, and other foreign volunteers, most of them members of Red Cross missions that travelled to Romania during the war. However, the vast majority of these medals went to women volunteers, most of them not professionally trained medical personnel. This public recognition and the

---

71 Cornea, *Insemnări*; Elena Negrescu, *Jurnal de război, 1916–1918* (Bucharest: Editura Detectiv, 2006).
72 Calypso Botez, *Problema feminismului: O sistematizare a elementelor ei* (Bucharest: Tipografia Guternberg S.A., 1920), 57.
73 See Mihăilescu, *Emanciparea*; Bucur, "Between Liberal and Republican Citizenship"; Cheșchebec, "Toward a Romanian"; Câncea, *Mișcarea*.
74 C. Hamangiu, *Codul General al României. Legi Uzuale*, Vol. 8 (Bucharest: Libraria Universală Alcalay & Co., 1926), 1064.
75 Ciupală, *Bătălia lor*, 192.

significant number of awardees could have become important data for demonstrating after the war that women had behaved patriotically, even heroically, in similar proportions as men: women had received 41 percent of the Queen Marie Crosses. Yet the only people who knew the total numbers were the military leadership and Queen Marie, and nowhere did either make public mention of these facts. The first to make public these impressive numbers was the book published by Alin Ciupală in 2017.

If this evaluation of Queen Marie comes off as harsh, it is in the context of the promises she made to Romanian feminists, the expectations of those activists, and the longer-term patterns of action and inaction the queen showed over her lifetime. Fiercely passionate about the things that were really dear to her, from Romanian irredentism in World War I to her horses and flowers, Marie spared no effort to achieve her goals. She showed no such passion and commitment to the feminist cause. As a reason, one might point towards the lack of familiarity between the queen and the parties closest to the suffrage cause, the socialists and the peasantists.[76] Before the war she had favored the Conservatives, who did not support women's enfranchisement. And the most powerful political figure of the early postwar years was Ion Brătianu, with whom the queen had a competitive relationship.[77] It may be that her charms were not effective on the leader of the National Liberal Party, which also did not favor women's enfranchisement.

There is no evidence the queen even tried to persuade the political leadership of the day. Had she wanted to do so, she had ample material to work with, from the selflessness demonstrated by thousands of women during the war as evidenced by the Queen Marie Cross to the studies, speeches, and legal precedents actively publicized by Romanian feminists during and immediately after the war. Women eventually gained limited voting rights in municipal elections in 1929 through the support of the Transylvanian-based National Peasant Party. Women's voting rights expanded only when Marie's son, Carol II, assumed royal dictatorship in 1938, handing them a powerless right. Marie played no role in this change and passed way several months later.

Conclusion

In providing a gender analysis of three faces of Queen Marie's activities during World War I—political, medical, and suffragist—this essay has critically assessed aspects of her biography that most other scholars of

---

76   Institutul Social Român, *Constituția din 1923*.
77   Ciupală, *Bătălia lor*.

the queen or the war have yet to connect.⁷⁸ My intent has not been to blacken the reputation of the queen or belittle her impressive contributions to the war. Yet most Romanian scholarly analyses touching on her contributions to the war and the several biographies that appeared outside Romania have avoided asking tough questions about the choices made by the queen and their impact on other Romanian women. Some have mistakenly identified her promotion of her own persona with a promotion of women's contributions to the war.⁷⁹ Others have seen her as representing attitudes and ideas that cannot be ascribed to her on the basis of any primary sources authored by the queen.⁸⁰

Fundamentally, my analysis asks one basic question: how does someone who wields power in gendered terms use (or not) that position of privilege for the benefit of others without power? During the war, Marie used this power to promote the Entente and irredentist goals with the Romanian king privately, and with the political and military leadership both publicly and also by proxy. She used her beauty and nursing costume ⁸¹ to raise large funds and spent much of her time modeling womanly support for the war effort in the hope of getting other women to become active in the same ways. She used her authority to bring some public recognition to these contributions through the Queen

---

78 Alin Ciupală's recent study is impressively comprehensive in its research, but does little to place its archival findings in any larger gender analysis of Romania at that time.
79 In the Romanian press, Ciupală's book has been seen as evidence of this. See Mihaela Mudure, "Printre feminisme," *Journal for the Study of Religions and Ideologies*, no. 6 (Winter 2003), http://www.jsri.ro/old/html%20version/index/no_6/mihaelamudure%20-%20articol.htm, accessed 16 September 2017. In a publication from 2016, out of four prominent scholars working on history or women's issues, three place queen Marie as number one in the "top five" of the most influential Romanian women in history. Two of them credit Marie with a "decisive diplomatic role in...accomplishing the Great Union [with Transylvania] in 1918" and respectively "the exceptional role she played during the Paris Peace Conference, in the United States and in Great Britain." The third commentator credits Marie with being "the main mobilizing factor of Romanian society during the war." See Alexandru Catalan, "Regina Maria, cea mai influentă româncă a tuturor timpurilor," *Click!*, 8 March 2016, http://www.click.ro/news/national/regina-maria-cea-mai-influenta-romanca-tuturor-timpurilor, accessed 16 September 2017.
80 The issue of Marie's love affairs with several men and the question of whether all of her children were Ferdinand's offspring has been an ongoing topic of speculation in a number of works that touch on her life. See Pakula, *Last Romantic*; Paul Quinlan, *The Playboy King: Carol II of Romania* (New York: Praeger, 1995).
81 I use the term "costume" to distinguish it from "uniform," because Marie was never an official member of any nursing unit. She wore these outfits for effect, just as she wore a red hussar outfit as an honorary officer of a cavalry unit. As she mentioned on several occasions in her autobiography, Marie was very fond of dressing up.

Marie Cross. But she never stood up publicly and forcefully in support of women's rights, either in the quest for suffrage rights or in other struggles for full civil rights or educational opportunities.

Illustration 4: The Monument of the Sanitary Heroes, Bucharest. Queen Marie is represented on a pedestal in the front of the base relief at the bottom of statuary ensemble showing a female figure symbolizing victory and two male soldiers, one fallen and the other crowned. Photo by Maria Bucur.

When the war was over, soldiers returned home with the promise of gaining land, which was eventually granted, and inhabitants of Transylvania were welcomed into the Romanian Kingdom with promises of full rights, which all men gained with the Constitution of 1923. However, women from all regions were left empty handed and told to return to their old roles, with no public long-lasting recognition of their wartime activities. They were told they needed to prove they were good mothers and wives and volunteer generously before they would garner support for political rights.[82] Until today, the only public memorial that provides any significant representation of women's contribution to the war is the Monument of the Sanitary Heroes in Bucharest (1932). The

---

82 Radu R. Rosetti, "Crucea Roșie," *Boabe de Grâu* 1, no. 9 (1930): 536–45.

large statue depicts two prominent female figures: an allegoric embodiment of Romania as victory (Nike), offering a crown of laurels to a male soldier, and a portrait of Queen Marie, standing on a pedestal as officers and un-named nurses look up to her in adoration. The time has come to take her off the pedestal and place her in historical context, next to and in relation to the experiences of millions of other women.

Stalinism and Anti-Stalinism in Romania: The Case of Alexandru Jar Revisited

Marius Stan and Vladimir Tismaneanu

Motto: "So we'd been lied when we're told that Tito is a hatchet man, or are we being lied today? Who is misleading us? And why? Who's mocking us? But a whole people? Why were we incited against this country of which we find out today that we are bound to it by a strong historical friendship?" (Alexandru Jar, 1956)

Abstract: *Communist writer Alexandru Jar (or Solomon Iacob, "Paşchela" for friends, 1911–1988) is the most prominent Romanian case of disenchantment with Stalinism. The 1956 "Jar Affair," as it came to be known in Romania and abroad, reveals the persistence of the Stalinist engagement of the Romanian communist leadership under Gheorghe Gheorghiu-Dej (1901–1965). By singling out Jar, a veteran party member and a former French Resistance fighter, the hegemonic nucleus within the Romanian Workers' Party succeeded in neutralizing political and intellectual challenges similar to those in Poland and Hungary. Based on newly discovered materials in the archives of the Romanian Communist Party's Central Committee, including Jar's party file and his numerous letters asking for political rehabilitation, this study offers a novel interpretation of the relationship between party leadership and intellectual unrest in Romania during the hectic year 1956. The authors explore the "Jar Affair" in a comparative, transnational historical perspective meant to highlight the complexities of political awakening in the aftermath of Nikita Khrushchev's Secret Speech. The article adds significantly to the understanding of the dialectics of de-Stalinization in East-Central Europe.*

Communist writer Alexandru Jar (or Solomon Iacob, "Paşchela" for friends, 1911–1988) is the most prominent Romanian case of disenchantment with Stalinism. The "Jar Affair," as it came to be known in Romania and abroad, reveals the persistence of the Stalinist engagement of the Romanian communist leadership under Gheorghe Gheorghiu-Dej. Mention should be made that during the Romanian Writers' Union Congress in April 1956, a series of interviews with communist writers, Jar's included, were published by the Union's journal *Gazeta literară*.[1]

---

1 Published in *Gazeta literară*, III/No. 15 (12 April 1956), 1.

Jar's liberalizing views expressed there were later deemed as "revisionist and anti-Party positions." He broached similar topics, in May 1956, in a meeting[2] of the party aktiv (cadres) of the district (*raion*) "I. V. Stalin,"[3] which took place at Floreasca Hall. He dared to speak out loud what many thought already, but did not have enough courage to articulate publicly. "A déclassé!," "A lumpen!," "A lunatic!"—this is what his former comrades in the communist clandestine groups and the French Resistance came to say about the one who, at the beginning of the 1950s, had been the scourge of socialist realism, the living proof for the internationalist claims of the Romanian Workers' Party, and widower to the famous militant Olga Bancic, a member of the French resistance group known as FTP-MOI (*Francs-tireurs et partisans—main-d'œuvre immigrée*), decapitated by the Nazis in Stuttgart, aged 32, in May 1944.

---

2   In brief, this is what Jar's Securitate file retains as details of the meeting: During those talks at the meeting of the party aktiv of the District Committee of the Romanian Workers Party "I.V. Stalin," "Jar embraced a revisionist and anti-Party position, advocating some ideas alien to the Party. Thus, he totally denied self-criticism and the class struggle, affirmed that the Party has been cultivating for years hypocrisy and fear, and implied that writers are being subjected to a permanent repression. He showed a great interest in a series of liberalist manifestations within other creators' unions from Poland, Czechoslovakia and Hungary, and he overrated some Western artistic 'values' while underrating values of our literature or the Soviet one. Speaking in plenum about the issue of satire, and related to his work 'Garagata,' which had been discussed and ultimately accepted for publication, Jar Alexandru [in communist official paperwork the surname precedes first name] said that 'in our country, the entire satire draws on greengrocery's and barber shop's level of complexity and topics, but the satire should be made not just for the puppies, but also for dogs.' And even on the national question Jar Alexandru had some ideas inconsistent with the party line, thinking that chauvinistic and racist ideas vanish along with the extinction of the enemy class. Jar himself has admitted after the meeting that 'the language and tone he had used in expressing all these anti-Party and libelous errors in front of the plenum are the effect of a low political level and a consciousness tainted by petty bourgeois individualism.' Based on the above briefly raised issues, Jar Alexandru had been expelled from the party." Source: CNSAS Archive, *Fond Informativ*, Dosar 187871, Vol. II, "Fișă personală," f. 8.

3   In 1950, the Great National Assembly passed a law dealing with a new administrative partition of the country. Thus, Bucharest, the capital, consisted of eight districts (*raioane*), named after Bolshevik luminaries, national historical figures of revolutionaries and other representative dates: "I. V. Stalin," "1 Mai," "23 August," "16 Februarie," "Tudor Vladimirescu," "Nicolae Bălcescu," "V. I. Lenin," and "Grivița Roșie." The district "I. V. Stalin" coincided with today's "Sector 1," North of Bucharest. This partition operated until 1968, when the districts became eight sectors, then six, after a new administrative reform in 1979.

The party aktiv meeting episode would be used for propaganda and psychological purposes, first and foremost as a deterrent against possible liberalizing temptations among Romanian intellectuals. Gheorghiu-Dej's ploy to identify the anti-Stalinist offensive with the much-compromised names of Alexandru Jar, Mihail Davidoglu, and Ion Vitner thus bore fruit. Add to this that the three were Jewish, thus helping the national Stalinist apparatchiks headed by Gheorghiu-Dej in their attempt to present themselves as true Romanian patriots opposed to liberal, cosmopolitan, and intellectualist tendencies.

Romanian intellectuals were not seduced by the Marxist revisionist rhetoric and saw the whole thing as no more than an internal party affair. Moreover, with the exception of a relatively small group of genuine leftist intellectuals (Petru Dumitriu, A.E. Bakonsky, Geo Dumitrescu, Eugen Jebeleanu, Geo Bogza, Paul Georgescu, N. Tertulian, Mihail Petroveanu, Gheorghe Haupt, and Ov. S. Crohmălniceanu), very few were able to understand the enormous stakes involved in the rearrangements taking place in 1956. None of them publicly expressed solidarity with the revolt of the Hungarian intellectuals (the influential novelist Petru Dumitriu was, in fact, among the first to lambast the Hungarian revolution in the pages of the Romanian Writers' Union's official weekly[4]). Leonte Răutu (1910–1993), a Bessarabian-Jewish hardliner who became a propaganda czar after Iosif Chișinevschi's removal in 1957, was able to simulate an ideological "opening" and basically succeeded in killing any liberalization in the egg.

The First Writers' Congress of 18–24 June 1956, manipulated by Leonte Răutu, then head of the Propaganda and Culture Department of the Central Committee of the Romanian Workers' Party, and his zealous underling, the Stalinist poet Mihai Beniuc, reaffirmed the principle according to which art and literature had to follow the party directives.[5] Of course, certain concessions were made, including the reintegration of some cultural values, long denigrated, into the political circuit.

The current historiography agrees with the fact that Alexandru Jar's case had been instrumentalized for a higher end and a higher

---

5   See "Referat prezentat de Direcția de Propagandă și Cultură prin care se aprobă proiectul de salut al CC al PMR adresat Congresului Uniunii Scriitorilor din RPR" (Memorandum of Agitprop for the Approval of the Draft of Romanian Workers's Party's Address to the Congress of the Writers' Union). The document was signed by Leonte Răutu and, besides the address, in which it was clearly stated that the socialist realism offered a variety of genres and styles for the development of writers' creativity, it also included a list of those who were to be elected to the leadership of the Writers' Union.

"prize": the political head of Miron Constantinescu. Historian Elis Pleșa, in her rigorously documented book on Gheorghiu-Dej's personality cult, spotlights Dej's scheme:

> the real target of the Romanian Workers' Party's leader had not been Alexandru Jar, but Miron Constantinescu, whom he [Gheorghiu-Dej] wanted to associate with the 'intellectualist and liberalist tendencies in the party'. As a matter of fact, the use of the 'Jar case' would come to light in only one year, at the Plenum [of the Central Committee] of June 1957, when Miron Constantinescu would be accused by Gheorghe Apostol of ties with 'that would-be writer Alexandru Jar', who already had been doomed by the party.[6]

In other words, what happened to Jar in 1956 was a set-up meant to stifle all "liberalizing" tendencies after Stalin's death, but mostly after Nikita Khrushchev's Secret Speech in 1956.

What we propose here, based on Alexandru Jar's Party and Securitate files (see footnote 30), different memoirs, other historical interpretations of the main events and protagonists, and our own work on and with the Romanian Workers' Party's historical records, is a thoroughgoing analysis of Jar's case and a reassessment of the significance of his "apostatical moment" in a broader transnational context. His political naivety notwithstanding (he wanted reforms by means of the Party), Jar decided to jump into the existential abyss created by the Secret Speech and that gesture needs to be pinned down in the nexus of major events related to 1956. He had no safety net and his fatal decision had been to mistaken the Romanian Workers' Party for the Polish United Workers' Party. In other words, there were no clearly delineated factions at the top of the Romanian Workers' Party and definitely there was no Władysław Gomulka ready and able to replace the well-versed schemer Gheorghiu-Dej.

Consequently, our article is just as much about Alexandru Jar as it is about Gheorghiu-Dej's cynical opportunism and devious political tactics. Studying Jar's file allows us to reassess the role of the Party Control Commission, of the Writers' Union, of some of the key-figures such as Gheorghiu-Dej, Leonte Răutu, Dumitru Coliu, Ion Vințe (János Vincze), Constanța Crăciun,[7] Pavel Țugui,[8] Mihai Beniuc, Mihai Novicov,

---

6   Elis Pleșa, *Gheorghe Gheorghiu-Dej. Cultul personalității* (Târgoviște: Editura Cetatea de Scaun, 2015), 144.
7   A Central Committee member, Minister of Culture, and Vințe's spouse, she served as a figurehead (member of the Council of State) under Ceaușescu. Born in 1914 in the city of Constanța, she passed away in 2002.
8   Extremely virulent as Leonte Răutu's deputy, notwithstanding his self-serving memoirs published after 1990.

Gheorghe Adorian,[9] Eugenia (Rosea) Luncaș,[10] Alexandru Buican-Arnoldi,[11] but also the meanings and the relevance of the cadre reports and of the autobiographies for what we call *the political culture of the communist ideocracy in Romania*.

If we were to compare Alexandru Jar to similar cases in Central Europe, we would suggest the names of Gyula Háy (1900-1975) in Hungary, and Adam Ważyk (1905-1982) in Poland. These intertwined biographical stories are telltale for what Peter Viereck once called "self-exorcism through projection," a case of people who were "equally sincere in both instances," Stalinist and anti-Stalinist. Speaking about Ważyk, with whom he had met in Warsaw in December 1962, Viereck draws on what actually constitutes the thrust of our article—a moral judgment: "To have made an honest mistake about Stalin, on the basis of misinformation and brainwashing for which one was not responsible, is no crime; to have evolved into a more independent person, drawing lessons from past errors, is on the other hand a positive merit."[12]

All these men experienced fully fledged Stalinism and had been unabashed apologists of a criminal dogma. Adam Ważyk who, in 1949, during the famous Fourth General Congress of Polish Writers "lauded some of Poland's older and established writers for their skill in adapting themselves to the artistic demands of the Party"[13] was the same Adam Ważyk who, in 1955, would write his *Poem for Adults*, one of the most remarkable documents of *awakening*. The former leading "true believer" Gyula Háy was the same Gyula Háy who in 1955 published *Why do I dislike Comrade Kucsera?*, that scathing text which foreshadowed the 1956 Hungarian revolution. We believe that it is only through such comparisons that we can start to understand and discern between reactions of guilt and opportunism in a time of crucial moral dilemmas and excruciatingly painful existential choices.

---

9   Péter Várady, Imre Tóth, *În viață sunt lucruri care nu se fac. Și care totuși se fac...* (Bucharest: Humanitas 2014).
10 She was a famous party old-timer and a close friend of Zina Brâncu's, the first rector of the Party School which would be known as "Ștefan Gheorghiu."
11 A hardened Comintern member, graduate of the "Leninist School" in the Former Soviet Union, and one of the leaders of the Romanian emigration to France; deported to Auschwitz, he then returned to Romania and worked as a minister councilor at the embassy in Belgrade before the break of the Soviet Union with the Yugoslav leader, Iosif Broz Tito.
12 Peter Viereck, *Strict Wildness: Discoveries in Poetry and History* (Piscataway, NJ: Transaction Publishers, 2008), 164.
13 Andrzej Franaszek, *Miłosz: A Biography* (Cambridge, MA: The Belknap Press of Harvard University Press, 2017), 266.

The Dramaturgy

Stalin's death was a political and psychological earthquake for all East European despots. They all tried to control and contain the centrifugal trends unleashed by the dramatic changes in the Former Soviet Union known as the *Thaw* (after the title of Ilya Ehrenburg's novella). Gheorghe Gheorghiu-Dej and his associates decided to abandon some of the most absurd industrial investments (for example, the Danube-Black See Canal) and allow for some relaxation in education and culture. However, the Romanian leader was the decisive factor behind the execution of his main political rival, Lucrețiu Pătrășcanu, in April 1954.[14]

To a great extent unwittingly, Alexandru Jar (1911–1988) found himself in the middle of a political maelstrom full of intrigues, innuendos, and travesties. Precisely because he had been so close to Gheorghiu-Dej, Jar committed political suicide by carrying out the leafer's enticing behests. It is likely that the vainglorious writer saw himself as a kind of intellectual maverick ignoring his lack of popularity among the Romanian writers and underestimating the cynical techniques used by Gheorghiu-Dej and his acolytes. Jar had been expelled from the Romanian Workers' Party based on the Party's (in fact Gheorghe Gheorghiu-Dej's) interpretation of his statements in 1956, and put under operative surveillance (*filaj*) by the former Securitate.[15]

In the aftermath of that 1956 episode, the regime would find out about private talks between Jar and other writers and artists from Jar's own friends acting as informers for the Securitate. In one such informative note dated 30 May 1959, the source "David" tells the secret police about Jar's discussions with painter and party member Gheorghe Labin, who has expressed discontent with the government's political arrests and convictions and said that communism does not make use of such methods. Based on the same source, the party finds out via Securitate that Jar assured Labin that things will change for the better for writers and artists in general, and he backs this belief with Khrushchev's speech content delivered at the Congress of Soviet writers (1954).[16] The Soviet leader had recommended to writers to be more humane and give a hand with the rehabilitation of those who had fallen into sin.

---

14 Vladimir Tismaneanu, *Stalinism for All Seasons. A Political History of Romanian Communism* (Berkeley & Los Angeles: University of California Press, 2003).
15 CNSAS Archive, *Fond Informativ*, Dosar 187871, Vol. II, "Fișă personală," f. 9.
16 Ibid., "Informative Note," f. 14.

In one of his self-critical recorded texts from his file, Jar admits to his errors and feels the need to re-emphasize the essential role played by the Propaganda and Culture Department and Leonte Răutu's constant support.[17] Lest we forget, the latter had been the one who led the decisive attack against Jar during that 1956 plenum. Jar tried to suggest that when he committed those errors he was thinking in the spirit of Mikhail Sholokhov's and Ilya Ehrenburg's speeches, delivered at the Second Congress of Soviet Writers in December 1954. During that period, "the thaw" in Soviet literature was again under attack, and Sholokhov and Ehrenburg had dared to call for more openness, honesty and "sincerity" in Soviet literature (although, on the other side, Sholokhov saw the latter's homonymous novel —*The Thaw*— as "an artistic step backwards"). What this confession proves is not Jar's internationalist outreach *per se*, but points to the watershed moment in his political apostasy. If that was façade or not, if his later repentance was façade or not can be discussed. But his *former God*'s death in March 1953, the Secret Speech in 1956 and the consecutive waves of shock onto different sub-scenes of political life, such as the writer's world, have had a huge emotional impact on former true believer Alexandru Jar.

From another informative note delivered to the Securitate by a certain agent "Petru Cercel" on 29 May 1956 (same day as the meeting) we find out that Jar had been completely in shock after that gathering. The note quotes one of Jar's aunts by marriage (accountant at the Philharmonic) and her vivid depiction of Alexandru's state of mind:

> "When we saw him, we got scared. He was washed-out, thin, pale, with the eyes of a madman; he had not been sleeping or eating for two days in a row. He kept on going around in circles, gesticulating frantically and trying to light one cigarette after another. 'Unbelievable... Extraordinary... Unreal', this was all he could say at the beginning. Then he told us that he never realized the 'trap' he had fallen into, not even when he got expelled from the Romanian Workers' Party's organization of the Writers' Union. There, he had brazened it out one more time by saying: 'I am the only communist among you, because I believe... You, you don't believe... You can expel me from whatever parties of the world, I am still a communist'."[18]

The relative then tells the Securitate agent that Jar had realized the seriousness of his new status only after reading an article in *Scînteia*, and that he deemed the entire situation as a misfortune, a side-effect to

---

17   Ibid., f. 17.
18   Ibid., f. 26.

the party's intentions to get rid of the old guard,[19] to re-establish a hardcore political line. So, Jar's thoughts, as recalled by his aunt, were: "Destalinization is a deep phenomenon which in the Union has led to the suicide of [Alexander] Fadeyev. It cannot be 'perverted' through yet another classic Stalinist method, a criticism based on throwing responsibility on others—against all evidence, and on some people designated as victims and scapegoats."[20]

The communist intellectual Alexandru Jar launched his explicit onslaught on the Stalinist practices in front of the regime's leaders, including Gheorghe Gheorghiu-Dej, the first secretary of the Central Committee of the Romanian Workers Party. It is highly important to notice that this episode took place just a few weeks after Nikita Sergeyevich Khrushchev's "Secret Speech" had been delivered behind closed doors on 25 February 1956, during the 20th Congress of the Communist Party of the Soviet Union, a smashing document which led to the explosion not just of Stalin's myth but of the whole monolithic unity of world communism. We are at the dawn of the centrifugal era, of what the Italian communist leader Palmiro Togliatti once called "polycentrism."[21] Jar was most likely unaware of the behind-the-scene intrigues and conspiracies which shattered Gheorghiu-Dej's absolute power. A genuine Leninist, he thought that a return to the original Bolshevik norms of party life, including collective rather than autocratic leadership, was the necessary path to be followed in order for the Party to regain the confidence of the masses.

Jar had been one of Gheorghe Gheorghiu-Dej's intimate friends, and quite often on the guest list at Dej's evening feasts at his residence on Boulevard I. V. Stalin or at the Central Committee's Swimming Pool. And it was Gheorghiu-Dej himself (who had known Jar from the time when they were in the Doftana prison together and still called him by his

---

19 In 1956, Gheorghiu-Dej was already convinced and even spelled out that Imre Nagy (1896–1958) should be "hung by the tongue." Two years later, in 1958, the Central Committee's Plenum would decide upon launching the witch-hunt against old party members accused of factionalism. The withdrawal of the Soviet troops from Romania in 1958 would not have happened if Dej had wavered in his unconditional support for the clampdown on the Hungarian revolution or had not proved himself as a loyal myrmidon of the Kremlin. And in full De-Stalinization process, he did it in full Stalinist fashion.
20 Ibid., f. 27.
21 Palmiro Togliatti, "Diversity and Unity in the International Proletarian-Communist Movement," in *Rinascita* [the media outlet of the Italian Communist Party], December, 1961; and Palmiro Togliatti, *Il memoriale di Yalta* (Palermo: Sellerio Editore, 1988)—originally written in August 1964 in Crimea during one of his holidays, the document represents Togliatti's "testamento politico."

original Jewish name, "Paşchela") the one who, when Jar embraced Khrushchevite revisionism and complained to him about the party dictatorship over literature and arts, had encouraged him to speak up and publicly express his discontent. According to Jar, Gheorghiu-Dej had urged him to say all that he had on his soul, to share with the Party his worries, inner doubts, and his wish for a radical change in dealing with cultural affairs.

The hyper-astute dictator found his storytelling skills amusing. He was among the very few who did not fear Iosif Chişinevschi,[22] Leonte Răutu[23] or the literary satrap Mihai Beniuc.[24] After all, he had his own revolutionary pedigree, much more impressive than that of various instructors within the Central Committee's Propaganda and Culture Department. He was an avid reader of printed media from different socialist countries, and was totally up-to-date with what was known as the *post-Stalinist thaw*. He uttered iconoclastic stances in that 1956 interview conducted by Mihail Petroveanu and published by *Gazeta literară*. Alexandru Jar was probably imagining himself as Romania's Adam Ważyk.

After all, the Polish poet had been himself an adamant Stalinist but that did not stop him from publishing in 1955 *A Poem for Adults (Poemat dla dorosłych)*, one of the most influential and impressive texts belonging to the literature of awakening from what Immanuel Kant called "dogmatic slumber."[25] During the years of virulent dogmatism, Jar was, together with Petru Dumitriu, the voice of the most aggressive form of socialist realism. The Party had charged the former with glorifying the Canal (see the novel *Drum fără pulbere/Road Without Dust*) and the latter with the encomiastic literary production meant to strengthen the myth of the heroic proletarian leader Gheorghiu-Dej. It is worth mentioning that in that period, Petru Dumitriu refrained from any dissenting allusions, and that in the years preceding his 1960 "defection" he had been working on a volume titled *Contemporary Biographies*, in

---

22 Cristian Vasile, *Politicile culturale comuniste în timpul regimului Gheorghiu-Dej* (Bucharest: Humanitas, 2011).
23 On Leonte Răutu's remarkable political versatility and prominent role within communist censorship, see Vladimir Tismaneanu and Cristian Vasile, *Perfectul acrobat. Leonte Răutu, măştile răului* (Bucharest: Humanitas, 2008).
24 Beniuc's memoirs have come out in 2016 in Romanian, although they cover distinct periods of time. See Mihai Beniuc, *Însemnările unui om de rând. Pagini de jurnal şi memorii (1965—1969; 1971; 1974)* (Cluj-Napoca: Editura Mega, 2016).
25 Immanuel Kant, Preface to *Prolegomena to Any Future Metaphysics* (London: Pearson Publishing, 1994).

which only his real literary talent distinguished him from the already relegated Jar's abject servility.

Nevertheless, in 1956 Alexandru Jar was wrong and the provocation succeeded. Jar was convinced that Gheorghiu-Dej really wanted him to embark on a soul-searching discussion of Stalinist abuses. In fact, selecting Jar, the beneficiary of a totally undeserved prominent literary status (he remained a committed socialist realist writer with no interest in literary experiments), to champion freedom of thought and expression was a masterstroke, indicative of Gheorghiu-Dej's and Răutu's sophisticated understanding of the game. Few writers were more despised among their peers than Jar was for his role in the Stalinist propaganda orgies. Having him appear as the voice of "liberalization" made the topic itself ridiculous for the majority of Romanian writers, who perceived it as a family quarrel among the Stalinists.[26]

More important, the aim of the setup was to compromise the potential "liberalizing" faction. The fact that Jar lacked the credibility to support his charges against Gheorghiu-Dej did not, needless to stay, mean that he was wrong. On the contrary, especially because it used party jargon and was imbued with references to Marxist-Leninist ideology, his attack, like those of other writers who supported him (all Jewish, all former firebrand Stalinists), was an assault on the party's ideological monopoly—indeed, a questioning of the regime's legitimacy. Miron Constantinescu, who was in Cluj, was called back for the meeting on Gheorghiu-Dej's orders. His presence was indispensable in discrediting Jar's "intellectualist-liberalist tendencies." It is essential to keep in the fact that Constantinescu had tried to give utterance to a sort of a Romanian Khruschevism in 1956. The 20th Congress of the Communist Party of the Soviet Union and the Secret Speech had made a tremendous impression on him. He would later be himself accused of factionalism, in 1957, and have his head for a washing following a Central Committee Plenum in 1961, when Gheorghiu-Dej, Ceaușescu, and Leonte Răutu made him and other old party members scapegoats for the initial stage of Stalinism in Romania.

---

26 The fact that Gheorghiu-Dej staged this provocation with Jar's unconscious help was revealed to one of the authors of this article (Tismaneanu) by Sorin Toma (1914–2016) in their private correspondence. After encouraging Jar to raise all his complaints during the meeting, Gheorghiu-Dej instructed Leonte Răutu and Miron Constantinescu to attack and discredit Jar. On the same topic, see Petre Pandrea, *Memoriile mandarinului valah. Jurnal 1954–1956* (Bucharest: Editura Vremea, 2011).

As such, Constantinescu, Gheorghiu-Dej, and Răutu, who were all part of the "communist Olympus" in 1956, and who normally would not have attended such a low-level meeting of party workers, were nevertheless present at this one and anathematized Jar, simulating a renewal of internal debate in the party. In the autarchic universe that was Romania in 1956, the publication of their speeches was also sensational in that they insisted on the party's decision to put an end to all Stalinist abuses.[27] What Constantinescu did not know at the time was that Dej has been planning to put him on a Party shelf and thus punish his iconoclastic tendencies. But Dej needed to prove something first and, at the same time, keep a close eye on all discussions around the Writers' Union and the intellectual circles in general. 1956 had been a watershed moment for the intra-party life throughout the Bloc.

Of course, Gheorghiu-Dej was no Bolesław Bierut, the ex-NKVD officer turned into the supreme leader of Sovietized Poland whose self-confidence had been so dramatically shaken by the New Course. And neither was the Romanian Workers' Party the Polish United Workers' Party, for at the top there was no (at least) vaguely reformist group. In April 1954, that is, a year and a month after Genialissimo Generalissimo's death,[28] the Politburo of the Romanian Workers' Party voted unanimously in favor of Lucrețiu Pătrășcanu's execution. In Romania, there was no Władysław Gomułka or Imre Nagy. Miron Constantinescu, Gheorghiu-Dej's future rival, had voted himself for the liquidation of the most talented among Romanian communist intellectuals and had been fully involved, as chairman of the State Planning Commission, in the activities of the Sovroms (Soviet-Romanian mixed companies), which had resulted in disastrous losses for the Romanian economy. Historian Ștefan Bosomitu published a remarkable biography of Miron Constantinescu where he explores the discussions on Stalinism and the Secret Speech at the top of the Romanian Workers' Party elite.[29] So, the humanist-democratic ideas of the Hungarian and

---

27 See the debate on the party *aktiv* of the I.V. Stalin, Bucharest, district committee of the Romanian Workers' Party, in *Scînteia*, 23 May 1956.
28 "Generalissimo of the Soviet Union" was a Soviet military rank specifically minted for Stalin in 1945 for "especially outstanding services to the Motherland in the management of all the Armed Forces of the state during the war." We elaborate on the formula "genialissimo generalissimo" in our homonymous co-authored volume: Marius Stan and Vladimir Tismaneanu, *Dosar Stalin. Genialissimul generalissim/A Stalin Dossier. The Genialissimo Generalissimo* (Bucharest: Curtea Veche, 2016; second edition).
29 Ștefan Bosomitu, *Miron Constantinescu. O biografie* (Bucharest: Humanitas, 2015).

Polish intellectuals had little counterpart in Romania. While writers in Poland and Hungary had started to assert themselves as an autonomous group, with well-defined interests and goals, in Romania there was a relative calm. At least publicly, all seemed quiet on the Romanian front. The Polish and Hungarian intellectuals acquired their rights after repeated conflicts with the ideological apparatchiks, which, considering the virulent forms of Stalinism in those countries, were not at all just a game. Every concession was won only by united resistance and public expressions of solidarity. Far from trying to synchronize their actions with those of their Hungarian and Polish peers, who were the avant-garde of the anti-totalitarian struggle, Romanian writers were happy with the very small degree of liberty offered to them after the death of Stalin.

During High Stalinism (1948–1953), nevertheless, Jar had been an arduous, passionate, indeed a hardcore Stalinist, non-hesitant, exalted, vehement, and aggressive. His books were simple, didacticist, bald and unexpressive. But he had that special status of paradigmatic illegalist, coming from the communist clandestinity and the shadows of the French Resistance. As he himself would recount in the numerous autobiographies he wrote during the 1950s and the 1960s,[30] he got himself to Paris in November 1937 sent by the Romanian Communist Party to write a novel titled *Grivița* (and it was in Paris that he started to work with the group dealing with dispatches to the International Brigades in Spain). The book never came out, but this commitment certainly mattered tremendously in his relationship with Gheorghiu-Dej, who treasured Alexandru Jar among his favorite mythographers. To a great extent, this also explains the dictator's rage when he found out that in private conversations after Stalin's death, his most trusted man had morphed into a "backbiter."

As a zealous supporter of the party line, the embodiment of Stalinist orthodoxy in the realm of literature, Jar would often times go to the "Mihai Eminescu" Literature School, an institution meant to educate young aspiring writers, where he would thunder and flash, in endless sessions, against the enemies of the people. He loved to stigmatize, to humiliate, to denounce any kind of imagined heresy. That is part of the reason why, encouraged by ideological czar Leonte Răutu, Gheorghiu-Dej had selected him to become the tribune of an implausible, even

---

30 Cordial thanks to historian Mihai Burcea for helping us with Alexandru Jar's party file (three volumes from the National Archives, Fond *53*) and his Securitate file (two volumes from the CNSAS Archives, Informative *Fond*).

impossible anti-Stalinism within the most Stalinist European communist party, with the exception, maybe, of Albania. In fact, it was a despot's revenge against the sycophant turned apostate. For Gheorghiu-Dej and Răutu it was obvious that the author of *Sfârșitul jalbelor* (*The End of Complaints*) could not become the catalyst of a serious intellectual revolt. His moral arguments did not have the aura of credibility on which people like Gyula Háy in Hungary and Leszek Kołakowski in Poland had built their iconoclasm.

This being said, Alexandru Jar was sincere in his disillusionment. He was neither a coward nor an opportunist. He had played his life on the communist card and he experienced Khrushchev's revelations as a personal trauma. The entire edifice of illusions, on which his whole life had been relying, suddenly appeared ruined to him. He had been a committed Stalinist, now he was equally sincere as an anti-Stalinist. His God had died, literally, and now figuratively.

So, he took the floor during that 1956 gathering, while Gheorghiu-Dej was verbally approving and inducing him not to end this emotional outburst of political disappointment and moral outrage. It was a well-planned, shrewd provocation and the impulsive Jar took the bait. Then there was an ominous break in the meeting. Gheorghiu-Dej's loyalist and much-feared ideological despot Leonte Răutu took the floor and exposed obsequiously sycophantic, embarrassing dedications which he personally had received from Jar along the years. This was the salvo for a cascade of accusations meant to completely and irrevocably annihilate Jar: Răutu evoked all possible sins, real or imagined. In this devastating portrait, Jar appeared as a literary mountebank, a charlatan, an egocentric, a lumpen, a megalomaniac, a despicable careerist. Of those present, only two writers, both terribly compromised themselves as former Stalinist hacks, timidly came to Jar's rescue: Ion Vitner (1914–1991), national poet Mihai Eminescu's main detractor, and Mihail Davidoglu, a mediocre playwright and author of the embarrassing play *Cetatea de foc* (*The Citadel of Fire*). The rest was just attack followed by yet another attack, renewed oaths of allegiance for comrade Gheorghiu-Dej and for the unbreakable unity of the party, viciously threatened by the petty bourgeois spirit embodied by the demonized Jar. This dramaturgy of anathematization was followed for weeks by stigmatizing meetings, in fact exorcising rituals, at the Writers' Union, and ruthless editorials in literary journals, first and foremost *Gazeta literară* (*The Literary Gazette*).[31]

The once acclaimed heroic combatant turned renegade practically ceased to exist overnight in the public space, although he was lucky enough not to be arrested. His books vanished from bookstores and libraries. Alexandru Jar's daughter became Dolores Bancic (instead of Jar). She continued to live within the Primăverii residential quarter of Bucharest, but he was forced to leave the sacred space of the nomenklatura and left Turgenev street for Aviator Mircea Zorileanu street (close to Cașin Monastery and the "Elias" Party Hospital). It is interesting to notice how Jar made constant appeals to the leadership of the Association of the Former Anti-Fascist Prisoners (AFDA) for some minor benefits (a pension increase or medical spas in various resorts). One medical report dated 11 July 1957, and signed by the main specialist, Medical School Professor Leon Caffé, prescribed a cure for asthenic neurosis in some "mid-altitude" mountain resorts like Bușteni or Poiana Țapului.[32] So the diagnostic decision had been taken by one of the members of the medical group associated with the Central Committee of the Romanian Workers' Party.

In 1960, Alexandru Jar addressed a memorandum to Gheorghiu-Dej in which he tried to justify himself and beseeched for the Party's forgiveness. He could not possibly conceive of his existence outside this messianic sect, which he gladly and enthusiastically had joined in the 1930s. The rejection of his request for readmission into the party happened unequivocally and inclemently in 1961.

In the aftermath of Gheorghiu-Dej's death, Jar was rehabilitated on 13 December 1967, and his party sanction was lifted. The readmission paper carries the signature of the same ideological inquisitor Dumitru Coliu, the one who had led the party investigation in 1956–1957. Jar published just a few books after he rejoined the Communist Party and died as a forgotten loner in November 1988, putting thus an end to a tragic saga of febrile beliefs intersecting, overlapping, and finally clashing with the iron logic of the ideological commissars. Sadly enough, the young generation of Romanian intellectuals barely resonates with Alexandru Jar's name anymore. His attempt at shaking the pyramid of dictatorial power had been nipped in the bud by Dej's backstage games

---

31 Luminița Marcu, *O revistă culturală în communism. Gazeta Literară, 1954–1968* (Bucharest: Cartea Românească, 2014).
32 For more details on Alexandru Jar's party life, see the Romanian National Archives (ANIC), Fond 53, "Arhiva CC al PCR," Dosar (de cercetare privind pe Alexandru Jar) Nr. 1101, Vol. I, II & III.

but also by the cowardice of his fellow comrades (from Ov. S. Crohmălniceanu and Maria Banuș, to Veronica Porumbacu and Paul Georgescu) who justified their capitulations and compromises during those fateful years by claiming that "Jar lacked talent." As if talent was his main problem...

In the mid-1950s, the works of the poets Octavian Goga, George Bacovia, and Tudor Arghezi, and the novelists Liviu Rebreanu and Camil Petrescu were once again allowed to circulate in Romania. Arghezi, who had been put in the shadow for ten years, was now rehabilitated: he agreed to sign the pact with that devil (the regime), and was allowed to publish again, which he, occasionally, also took as an opportunity to plaster the Party with praise. At the same time, the party bureaucracy tried to cultivate the myth of respect for the fundamental values of the past, remaining completely quiet about the fact that it was itself responsible for the abuse of those values. Breaking with hard-core Stalinism and rehabilitating national history were vital: in Romania, however, they were not the result of activities championed by critical intellectuals, but rather an opportunistic attempt on the part of the party elite to disguise its unwillingness to engage in real de-Stalinization.[33] But the regime even went so far as to try to attract back prominent Romanian intellectuals in exile, such as Mircea Eliade and Emil Cioran.[34]

The harsh treatment administered to a celebrated veteran party member like Jar was a signal that there was no intention nourished by Gheorghe Gheorghiu-Dej and his acolytes to allow for a Romanian-style Thaw. In March 1956, Dej had been challenged by Politburo members Iosif Chișinevschi and Miron Constantinescu and urged to assume personal responsibility for the abuses of the early 1950s. With the help of his trusted colleagues, former members of his entourage in the Doftana Prison and the Târgu-Jiu concentration camp (Gheorghe Apostol, Chivu Stoica, Nicolae Ceaușescu, Alexandru Drăghici, as well as

---

33 For the attempts to rewrite the history of Romania in the post-Stalinist period, see communist literary historian Pavel Țugui's *Istoria și limba română în vremea lui Gheorghiu-Dej: Memoriile unui fost șef de secție a CC al PCR* (*The Romanian History and Language under Gheorghiu-Dej*) (Bucharest: Editura Ion Cristoiu, 1999).

34 Marieta Sadova, a theater director who had moved in the same circle as Mircea Eliade and Emil Cioran in the interwar period, but had remained in Romania after the war and had been co-opted by the communist regime, was sent to Paris to contact them. Although she was asked to do this by Constanța Crăciun, then minister of culture, and Pavel Țugui, head of the culture section of the Central Committee between 1956 and 1960, it was used against her during a trial in February 1960, in which a larger group of intellectuals was also involved. See Țugui, *Istoria și limba română în vremea lui Gheorghiu-Dej*.

Alexandru Moghioroş), Gheorghiu-Dej deflected the attack, obtained a majority on the Politburo, and branded his critics as promoters of an anarchic spirit with the party. In June 1957, Chişinevschi and Constantinescu were denounced as factionalists and nostalgics of Ana Pauker's dogmatism, and lost their positions on the Politburo and the state apparatus (at that moment they were both vice-chairmen of the Council of Ministers). Once these two main figures were eliminated, chances for Khrushchev-style reforms in Romania became virtually nil.[35]

In November 1956, the Hungarian Revolution further confirmed Dej's conviction that de-Stalinization could lead to the regime's breakdown. As such, the wind of liberty of 1956 and the struggle for liberalization in Poland exasperated Stalin's Eastern European disciples, including Gheorghiu-Dej and his henchmen. Jar's calls for frankness and open debates were just the drastic indication of what the leaders diagnosed as the loss of party-mindedness and capitulation into the morass of petty-bourgeois "liberalism." This negative pedagogy consisted of the simple behest: If you don't want to share Jar's fate, don't walk into his footsteps.

The Jar case, the purging of the Writer's Union, the anti-revisionist fulminations of the Romanian literary press, and the furious diatribes of Mihai Beniuc against the humanist manifestos of the Hungarian and Polish intellectuals illustrate the specificity of the Romanian political elite's reaction to the de-Stalinization process going on in the other communist states. The denunciation of the poet Nicolae Labiş at the Young Writers Congress and the perfidious attack of Mihai Beniuc, stage-managed by Leonte Răutu, were obviously seen as warnings to calm radical passions.[36] However, unlike in Hungary or Poland, what the Romanian intellectuals did not have in 1956 was the support of a reform-oriented faction at the top of the party bureaucracy. While the Hungarians could count on Imre Nagy and his comrades and the Poles on Władysław Gomułka and his group, the few potentially heretical writers in Romania lacked any such protectors. Lucreţiu Pătrăşcanu had been executed in April 1954, and Miron Constantinescu was too isolated within the leadership of the Romanian Workers' Party to become the

---

35 Ghiţă Ionescu, *Communism in Romania. 1944—1962* (London: Praeger, 1976).
36 Among the vocal critics of Stalinist asphyxiation of the intelligentsia was the radiant young poet Nicolae Labiş. Attacked by Mihai Beniuc, himself manipulated by Leonte Răutu, Labiş continued to publish poems indicating disaffection with Stalinism and calling for a renewal of socialism in Romania along humanist lines, such as *Legenda pasiunii defuncte/The Legend of Defunct Passion*. Information provided to Vladimir Tismaneanu by Tita Chiper-Ivasiuc.

promoter of an anti-Stalinist campaign. All he could do was test the water and launch a few feelers, minor disagreements with Gheorghiu-Dej that were later treated as terrible crimes against the party's leading role. There was some ferment within the party old guard, but no collective efforts ever succeeded in fundamentally jeopardizing the Stalinists' grip on power.

Epilogue

Jar's nemesis, Leonte Răutu remained a candidate Politburo member (*membru supleant al Biroului Politic*) and head of the Propaganda and Culture Department until Gheorghiu-Dej's demise in March 1965. In 1964, when the Romanian Workers' Party took an increasingly anti-Soviet position and issued its April Declaration concerning the polemics within the international communist movement, Răutu excelled in a staunch criticism of the previous "Sovietization of the Romanian culture" (perpetrated, of course, under his enthusiastic guidance). Born Lev Oigenstein to a middle class Bessarabian Jewish family in Odessa, Răutu had joined the Romanian Communist Party underground in the early 1930s and became the editor of the party's newspaper *Scînteia*. During World War II, he worked as the head of Radio Moscow's Romanian Service. He returned from Soviet political exile in 1945 and became a main figure in the ideological apparatus. He was an expert survivor, a masterful chameleon, with a proverbial ability to engage in political somersaults.

In the early 1950s, he used Alexandru Jar as his instrument and, once the writer started to express doubts, Răutu concocted the libretto of his political and moral destruction. Under Ceaușescu, Răutu continued to hold influential positions, served as Central Committee secretary, Political Executive Committee member, and rector of the "Ștefan Gheorghiu" Party Academy. He lost all his positions in 1981 when one of his daughters applied for leaving definitively the country. Mihai Beniuc (1907–1988), the ultra-zealous head of the Writers' Union was ousted in February 1965 after he had criticized Gheorghiu-Dej's anti-Soviet course. In his memoirs (see footnote 24), Beniuc wrote contemptuously about Dej and his ideological servant Răutu.

Mihail Petroveanu, the author of the interview with Alexandru Jar mentioned in our article, died, together with his wife Veronica Porumbacu, in their apartment during the Bucharest earthquake on 4 March 1977. After his election as Gheorghiu-Dej's successor, Nicolae Ceaușescu rehabilitated many of his former patron's victims, including

Lucrețiu Pătrășcanu, Miron Constantinescu, Constantin Doncea, and, directly linked to our topic, Alexandru Jar. Yet, Romanian letters had benefited from the post-1965 relative opening, socialist realism had been abandoned as the mandatory artistic style, and Jar's less than modest literary gifts had no chance to ensure him any prestige. He remained confined to the periphery of literature, ignored and forgotten, a sad living testimonial of the times of Stalinist darkness.

In brief, the Jar Affair offered the Romanian Workers' Party top leaders an opportunity to reassert ideological control over art and literature, to conduct a veritable witch-hunt against real and imagined unorthodox intellectuals, to get rid of Gheorghe Gheorghiu-Dej's critics, and to avoid the coalescence of challenges, nuclei of critical thought such as the Petofi Circle in Hungary. The topic matters since it shows the methods used to resist de-Stalinization while pretending to draw the lessons from the main teachings of the Communist Party of the Soviet Union's 20th Congress. In our view, these tactics were similar to those used by Enver Hoxha in Albania.[37]

---

37   Elidor Mëhilli, *From Stalin to Mao: Albania and the Socialist World* (Ithaca: Cornell University Press, 2017), 86–90.

Katherine Verdery, My Life as a Spy: Investigations in a Secret Police File. Durham and London: Duke University Press, 2018. 323 pages.

Review by Radu Cinpoes, Kingston University, London, UK

The collapse of communism in the Eastern Bloc has prompted numerous investigations on the mechanisms of coercion and control of repressive regimes. Information on the former Securitate (the Romanian intelligence services) has emerged in earnest with the founding of the National Council for the Study of the Securitate Archives (CNSAS) in 1999. A number of important works exposing Securitate practices have appeared since.

It is in this context that Katherine Verdery's latest book – *My Life as a Spy: Investigations in a Secret Police File* – is published in 2018. The book is divided into two parts. One reconstructs the author's research journey to Romania in the 1970s and 1980s, piecing together information from her Securitate file, research field notes and personal letters. The other draws on information from the file and from interviews with informers and Securitate officers in a journey of understanding the mechanisms and impact of surveillance.

Verdery weaves together these narratives, but the construction appears, at times, to be bursting at the seams. This is an assumed risk, which the author acknowledges in the Prologue. The gains, however, make the book stand out in the field of secret police surveillance. Juxtaposing auto-ethnography, ethnography, memoires and a critical appraisal of all these allows for several levels of analysis. Firstly, the minute depiction of the Securitate operations captures various idiosyncrasies and fixations of the regime (such as the hierarchical dynamics between the rural, urban and central levels of the Securitate, the compartmentalisation of operations, the obsession with the Hungarian threat, etc.). Here, the value lies primarily in the richness of the information (from the author's own confession, hers was one of the most voluminous files from all the others kept on American citizens under Securitate surveillance). This quantitative 'advantage' is skilfully exploited, adding to the existing body of evidence on the Romanian secret police practices. It is with the other layers, however, that this book truly brings value and nuance.

A second layer of reading concerns the contrasting realities emerging from the author's examination side-by-side of her field notes and memories, the informant notes and the Securitate reports. The dissonant selves constructed in these documents point to an identity crisis with which Verdery is wrestling throughout the book. These multiple selves (Kathy – 'the novice ethnographer'; 'the Folklorist' – the spy targeting military secrets in rural Romania; 'Vera' – the pro-Hungarian spy in Cluj; Katherine Verdery the successful American Professor and 'Vanessa' – under surveillance in the US) become a house of distorted mirrors. To exit this maze, the author has to find herself by examining all the facets of her personality that these 'reflections' produce. The fact that Verdery seriously asks herself whether she could have been considered a spy speaks for the effectiveness of the surveillance mechanisms and the sense of alienation and self-doubt that they meant to raise in the 'objectives' (a dehumanising appellative facilitating the isolation of the person under investigation from their social circles). Using the word 'spy' without quotation marks in the title emphasises – as the author indicates – this 'fluidity' of self-perception (p.5).

Thirdly, the examination of the Securitate reports and her own field notes provokes another revelation: the similarity between the work of the ethnographer and that of the Securitate operative. This produces a depressing sense of self-doubt, reinforcing the identity crisis. Verdery struggles to resolve this crisis: the mitigating factor – despite both being in the business of collecting information about people's lives – is that in the ethnographer is guided by clear ethical principles, while the Securitate operative by deceit and secrecy.

Fourthly, the author's conversations with friends and acquaintances who appear as informants in her Securitate file raise important moral questions about the often-blurred lines between perpetrators and victims. While going through expected phases of disappointment, betrayal and rage, Verdery does not fall into the trap of default-blaming people who informed on her. Instead, she engages in a nuanced examination of the role she inadvertently played in creating difficult contexts for people leading to their recruitment by the Securitate. However, the attempt to understand and exculpate her informers comes at a price: self-blame. Mariana's statement – 'what a lot of harm you caused me!' (p.238) – and the subsequent soul-searching it triggers for Verdery brings the complexity of the relationship between the informers and their victims to the fore. The author manages to somewhat transcend the self-blame process and through understanding comes the possibility for reconciliation.

Finally, facing some of the Securitate officers involved in her case enables Verdery to consider the dynamics between informers, secret police operatives and targets. The ethnographic analysis of social circles and norms that guide interaction in Romania provides the basis for understanding. This is intertwined with a more subjective perspective: the authors confesses to almost having 'crushes on these men' (p.262), another reason for self-doubt pointing to the effectiveness of the Securitate. Her statement that the Securitate 'definitely knew how to select people who could make a good human connection' (p.262) comes close to rehabilitating these individuals. Verdery accounts for the human dimension of the Securitate apparatus, but remains a staunch critic of the secret police in Romania – a more nuanced and tempered one, who makes no claims of having acquired an absolute understanding of the Securitate, its role and effects on Romanian society.

The strained stitching together of the different parts notwithstanding, the book is an invaluable and novel contribution to the field. The levels of analysis and the important questions about surveillance, ethnographic research, identity, guilt and victimhood and about social relations more generally appeal to a wide range of audiences. For those with no extensive knowledge of communist Romania it provides a detailed initiation into the workings of the secret police. For academics and experts in the field, it provides a rich source of information and a challenge to reconsider their own positions with regards to the issues it addresses.

Cristian Vasile ed., "Ne trebuie oameni!": Elite intelectuale şi transformări istorice în România modern şi contemporană. Târgovişte: Editura Cetatea de Scaun, 2017. 442pp.

Review by Roland Clark, University of Liverpool, UK

Modern Romania has transitioned from feudal principalities to a nation-state, from the Old Kingdom with its limited suffrage to democratic Greater Romania, from a constitutional monarchy to Ion Antonescu's military dictatorship via the royal dictatorship and the National Legionary State, then into various stages of state socialism and post-socialism. How have intellectual elites shaped the country's sometimes radical regime changes, and how have individual careers been cut short or redirected by these 'historical transformations'? The case studies contained in *"Ne trebuie oameni!"* (*"We Need People!"*) follow the changing fortunes of intellectuals, specialists, or ideas through one or more regime changes. While doing so, the book traces the "processes of producing new languages of knowledge" (p. 12), differing approaches to professionalization, and how various regimes define "intellectuals" and "elites."

Six of the seven case studies are structured around individual or collective biographies. The biographical approach allows the authors to use individuals as a "red thread" that connects seemingly very different regimes together. Tracing individual lives might mean emphasizing continuities rather than ruptures, but what this volume demonstrates is how difficult it was for individuals to negotiate the transition from one regime to another. Most of those who did pursue prominent careers across two regimes frequently only did so by renouncing deeply held beliefs and/or by rejecting their key intellectual contributions from an earlier period. The only non-biographical chapter, by Cristian Vasile, focuses on the fluctuating meanings of "modernity" and "modernization" before and during state socialism. He demonstrates that whereas successive regimes prior to 1944 framed their ambitions in terms of "modernization," communists of the 1940s and 1950s preferred to speak of "progress" and "development." Instead of "modernization, the communists wanted an "unconditional spectrum of social progress, facilitating the flowering of the forces of production, science, art, and culture." (p. 292) "Modernization" reappeared in communist discourse during the mid-1960s, now shaped by influences from American political science.

Ionuț Biliuță's study of four nineteenth century Orthodox clergymen argues that his subjects "formed a direct opposition to the attempts of the state to prevent the unification of the Principalities, thus inaugurating a new form of Orthodox clerical political activism: nationalist opposition to the retrograde conservatism of a state subordinated to the Ottoman and tsarist empires." (p. 27) As Romanian nationalists, these hierarchs found themselves in conflict with their Greek counterparts, whose ties to Constantinople made them bitter opponents of the planned nation-state. Biliuță argues that the Romanians were able to reject Caesaropapist arguments about subordination to the Ottoman state thanks to the influence of Western Enlightenment ideas about education, professionalization, and the nation which had already permeated Romanian Orthodox circles. Călin Cotoi's chapter reiterates the importance of Western influences. Focusing on debates over how to best combat cholera epidemics, Cotoi emphasizes that when Romanian doctors and public health officials battled over the relative merits of quarantine zones or bacteriology, they framed their arguments in terms of modernity and racial degeneration. They did so within a transnational community of specialists, and Cotoi makes the provocative argument that "the establishment of the modern Romanian state is a result, at least in part, of European and Russian worries about epidemics." (p. 74) Cholera in Romania threatened the health of the rest of Europe, and the survival of elites and institutions in the face of new scientific discoveries and a changing geopolitical situation depended on how well they were able to prevent the spread of disease.

Chapters by Valentin Săndulescu and Camelia Zavarache focus on the interwar period and the transition into a Communist state. As Săndulescu notes, a number of young intellectuals affiliated themselves with the fascist Legion of the Archangel Michael during 1932-33 and tied their careers directly to the movement. Some lost their lives during Carol II's regime, but the survivors found prestigious jobs under the National Legionary State. Legionary intellectuals used their power to promote their own interests and to persecute their enemies, but when the regime collapsed five months later many were dismissed, imprisoned, or both. Săndulescu demonstrates that some nonetheless survived both Antonescu and state socialism through "radical professionalization," or by "retreating into a strictly specialized area" where they were "sheltered from public visibility, excessive political influence and, implicitly, the potential for repressive measures." (p. 173) Surviving state socialism was difficult for intellectuals on the left as well as the right. Zavarache's study of three left-wing psychologists, Mihai Ralea, Alexandru Roșca, and Mihai

Beniuc, before and after the rise of the communism confirms many of Săndulescu's conclusions about transition. Establishing important research centres in Cluj and Iași during the 1930s and then being marginalized for their communist sympathies during the war, all three successfully integrated into the socialist state, but not without significant intellectual compromises, suspicion, and denunciations.

Anca Șincan's analysis of the corruption trial of Gheorghe Nenciu, the director of the Department of Cults, in 1977 shows that even people who appeared to be "perfect" communists still carried pre-war baggage. Șincan argues that Nenciu was purged for cultivating behaviors that had been characteristic of church officials *prior* to the rise of communism and which had never properly been eradicated. The regime's desperate need for specialists had allowed people with questionable pasts to survive and it was not until 1977 that the Party was independent enough to purge them. Finally, Narcis Tulbure sheds light on the scandalous manipulation of economic statistics in 2014 by explaining how communist approaches to statistical data were diametrically opposed to the ways Western economists used it. Whereas in the West statistics formed the basis of economic planning, under state socialism they were a state secret and a way for specialists "to negotiate power relations" by using them "as practical manifestations of the limits of legibility and opacity." (p. 375) Collectively, these chapters challenge us to rethink our assumptions about how interconnected Romania's past actually was.

Ioana Em. Petrescu & Liviu Petrescu, Scrisori Americane *(1981-1983)*, Ediție îngrijită, studiu introductiv, notă asupra ediției și note de Ioana Bot, postfață de Liana Vescan. Cluj-Napoca: Casa Cărții de Știință, Cluj-Napoca, 2017, 366 pp.

Review by Iuliu Rațiu, Babeș-Bolyai University, Cluj-Napoca, Romania

In a letter sent on 23 March 1983, during her two-year stint as a Fulbright scholar at UCLA, Ioana Em. Petrescu tries to humor her friend Georgeta Antonescu from Cluj, Romania, with anecdotes from sunny California. Responding to Antonescu's distress about fulfilling her duties at the university in Cluj while tending to the poor health of her mother, Petrescu turns her friend's attention to motivational feel-good American stories--the newly found mantra of "life begins at forty," the benefits of jogging during rain, and the *Los Angeles Times' Dear Abby* advice column. Then, Petrescu jokingly compares two so-called national sports, *standing in line* and *jogging*, predicting that one could never replace the other. For Petrescu, coming from communist Romania, where everybody but the party elites spent countless hours standing in line to buy food, jogging was the ultimate pastime.

Petrescu's joke about *jogging* and *staying in line* describes the social, economic, and cultural divide between Romania and the United States during the Cold War. Petrescu, her friends and her family knew well that the fearful secret police *Securitate* could intercept their correspondence and that is why innuendoes and wordplays had better be kept unwritten. Even so, *jogging* represented an affluent and free society, always on the move, while *staying in line* embodied a society frozen in time, wherein almost everybody had to literally and figuratively stay in line in order to survive. Thus, colorful California was portrayed as the opposite of colorless Romania. When Americans did their best just to step out of line, Romanians were aware that the smallest of steps out of line would put them in danger.

The letter is part of Ioana Em. Petrescu and Liviu Petrescu's recently published correspondence volume *Scrisori Americane (1981-1983)*. Liviu Petrescu's name is mentioned on the cover both because occasionally he cosigned his wife's letters and because a handful of his own letters are excerpted in the book. Showcasing both the excitement and the difficulties of international academic exchanges in communist Romania, the letters present scholars from behind the Iron Curtain navigating the pros and cons of life in the free world. While the

Petrescus are happy to be away, they are also worried about the family and friends they left behind. In the introductory study, Ioana Bot writes that Petrescu did not intend to publish her letters but instead wanted to use them as first drafts for a travelogue she hoped to write about her American stay. Petrescu passed away before completing the travel book but her letters, together with some official documents referenced in the afterword by Liana Vescan, the librarian in charge of the Petrescu Family archive, retrace her geographical and spiritual journey.

The personal rawness of the letters is only rivaled by the absurd cruelty of the bureaucratic hurdles Romanian recipients of Fulbright scholarships had to go through during communism in order to benefit from the experience. Read side by side, the award letter signed by an American administrator of the Council for International Exchange of Scholars (CIES) and a Romanian Education Ministry affidavit signed by Petrescu reveal the fact that Romanian Fulbright scholars had to donate two-thirds of their daily allowance to the Romanian state. That was the price Romanian academics had to pay for the tall order of conducting research abroad.

Despite pecuniary shortcomings, bitterly felt in the land of rampant consumerism, the letters address steady and well-deserved spiritual and intellectual gains. Written with a small audience in mind, the correspondence maps out Petrescu's private and professional life. Constantly concerned about the well-being of her loved ones, the academic covers topics ranging from the price of groceries or her culinary skills to street fashion or academic trends. She writes about the museum she visits, the students she mentors, and the professional functions she attends. Because Petrescu describes the same events to both her mother and her best friends, the information is repetitive but never redundant since it both frames and edits reality according to the audience to which the letters are intended. For instance, when she writes to her mother, Petrescu never mentions her occasional health problems, her greying hair, or her husband's losing weight. But when she writes to her friends, she constantly alludes to her and her husband's depressive moods and overpowering worries concerning their financial instability, the possibility of not getting funding for a second year, or the lack of news from home.

This framing mechanism by which Petrescu selectively edits in or out the negative side of her American experience emphasizes the positive aspects. These are the true gains of the Petrescus' stay in California, which the writer shares with all her correspondents. First, there is the direct contact with an open and competitive education system, enthusiastic students, open-stack libraries, and the international Fulbright scholars. Then, there are the professional accomplishments, such as the successful preparation and teaching of various Romanian language, literature, and culture courses (which were actual mentorship programs due to low enrollment in the Romanian Studies program at UCLA) or the organization of a month-long joint event dedicated to celebrating the Bulgarian and Romanian cultures. In his turn, Liviu Petrescu, an academic himself, conducted independent research and was occasionally invited to lecture about contemporary Romanian novels. Last, there are the small personal achievements, such as cooking *sarmale* for the American students, exploring Los Angeles and California, and living in the US for two years at the beginning of the most brutal decade of Ceaușescu's Romania.

After reading these letters about the American experience of an academic couple, one can only wonder what a travelogue written by Petrescu herself might have looked like. As such, the letters are an important life document and might be of value to those analyzing biographical writing or are interested in conducting research about academic exchanges during the Cold War.

Bruce O'Neill, The Space of Boredom. Homelessness in the Slowing Global Order. Durham and London: Duke University Press, 2017, 253 pages.

Review by Petru Negura, Free International University of Moldova, Chisinau, Moldova

Bruce O'Neill's book proposes an anthropological analysis of the social environment of homeless people in Bucharest from the perspective of boredom. The topic might surprise the readers, both specialists and neophytes. Homeless people endure multiple deprivations – lack of a domicile and a stable income, a fragile social support, often addictions, and generally low education levels. Not having a stable home or a job could in itself induce an acute feeling of stress, stimulated by the instinct of survival – a state hardly comparable to boredom. Very few researchers have approached the feeling of boredom in relation to homelessness.

The book unveils the otherwise hidden world of homeless people living in Bucharest, going beyond a photographic representation of this environment. Anthropological research and analysis tools help the author – and the reader – to understand the "indigenous" meanings produced and used by the homeless. An outsider could overlook many aspects central to their daily experience. One of these is the boredom that grinds their mood and existence. To understand the significance of this feeling, O'Neill immerses himself in the daily experiences of the Bucharest homeless with whom he spends time to communicate, eat and get bored around a day center, the shelter, and the squatter camps. The author crosses the city by taking the routes and visiting the places frequented daily by his research participants, drinking coffee in gas stations near the day center, waiting early in the morning for potential employers, discussing with sex workers at the railway station and amusing himself with users of the day center in a large store on the outskirts of Bucharest. O'Neill is particularly interested in the practical dimension of boredom as a complex experience of rupture, of displacement from a range of resources that most people take for granted: home, work, family support, and social recognition. As O'Neill shows, a main trigger of boredom for the homeless is their material inability to respond to the social pressure to consume and participate in Bucharest's enormous consumer goods market.

With the help of a complex theoretical apparatus and in-depth familiarity with the recent history of Romania, O'Neill tries to decipher in daily routines large-scale change that turned that country into a participant in the global consumer market. Homeless people occupy a marginal position in a country that is struggling to overcome its peripheral status. In a country where success is defined by living, working and consuming in an alert rhythm, the inability to keep the pace is expressed emotionally through the sense of existing in slow-motion. Sporadic access to some forms of consumption by some of the homeless – seasonal workers, day-laborers, or sex workers – gives them the sense of living "authentic." A chocolate, a coffee or a beer become the momentary symbols of a jump from the tedious and worthless existence of a homeless to "another life" that is nothing but a simulacrum of an otherwise inaccessible "normality." Similarly, sex with male sex workers in the public restroom of the railway station appears as a makeshift, as Tova Höjdestrand put it, of satisfaction in a global economy of desire.

The author seeks to delimit the meaning of this feeling of boredom. As he explains, the boredom felt by the poorest of Bucharest is fundamentally different from the Marxist idea of alienation of the workers in a repetitive workload. The workers can at least spend their after-work free time with their fellows and family, according to the cultural norms of their time and environment, but the homeless are bored continuously. Boredom is different from depression in its clinical, individual dimension. Homeless people in Bucharest are to be understood as a "reserve army of labor," to use another Marxist term, a class of redundant people in an economic and political system based on competition and consumption. Their boredom also comes from the sense of personal uselessness and irrelevancy when reduced to non-existence in economic and social terms. At the same time, both the homeless and the domiciled people belong to the same mental universe and social configuration, and have the same false consciousness making them believe that the capitalist, consumer society is the only legitimate one.

The Space of Boredom is also a plea for solidarity in an anomic society, in the sense of Durkheim, where a moral order based on mutual help and a sense of community is being disrupted by individual struggles for a better place in a profit-based system. Here the feeling of uselessness felt by the homeless is analogous to the "not neededness" that Höjdestrand discusses in her book on homelessness in Russia, a feeling defined by the cultural need to help the others. A solidarity-based system gives everyone a chance not only to "count on" others, but also to "count for" helping others (S. Paugam). In this respect, institutions providing services to homeless people, including those discussed in the book, alienate their users because they do not create networks of solidarity and mutual support.

The book does not reduce the lives of the homeless to a negative sense of helplessness, but through boredom explores the marginalization of homeless people in a world that refuses them the chance to be and to feel helpful. At a closer look, boredom is not only a destructive feeling because it creates new frames of sociability, solidarity, and sometimes carnivalesque rebellion. *The Space of Boredom* is more than a book about homeless people in a Southeastern European city, it is a thorough and systematic reflection on suffering, exclusion and solidarity in a society rushed to overcome its marginality.

Bruce O'Neil's book will certainly be a revealing and exciting reading for scholars, students and an intellectual public interested in the impact of the Romanian post-socialist transition towards globalized capitalism over the most deprived and vulnerable.

AST EUROPEAN STUDIES: JOURNALS AND BOOK SERIES

Soviet and Post-Soviet Politics and Society

Editor: Andreas Umland

Founded in 2004 and refereed since 2007, SPPS makes available, to the academic community and general public, affordable English-, German- and Russian-language scholarly studies of various empirical aspects of the recent history and current affairs of the former Soviet bloc from the late Tsarist period to today. It publishes approximately 15–20 volumes per year, and focuses on issues in transitions to and from democracy such as economic crisis, identity formation, civil society development, and constitutional reform in CEE and the NIS. SPPS also aims to highlight so far understudied themes in East European studies such as right-wing radicalism, religious life, higher education, or human rights protection.

Journal of Soviet and Post-Soviet Politics and Society

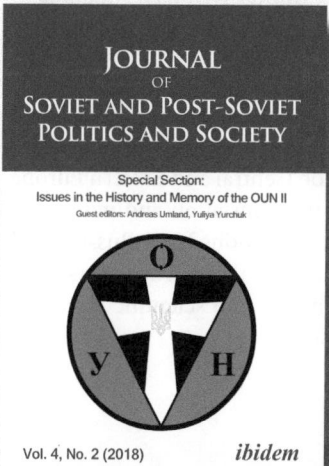

Editors: Andreas Umland, Julie Fedor, Andrey Makarychev, George Soroka, Tomasz Stępniewski

The Journal of Soviet and Post-Soviet Politics and Society is a new bi-annual journal that was launched in April 2015 as a companion journal to the Soviet and Post-Soviet Politics and Society book series (founded 2004 and edited by Andreas Umland, Dr. phil., PhD). Like the book series, the journal will provide an interdisciplinary forum for new original research on the Soviet and post-Soviet world. The journal aims to become known for publishing creative, intelligent, and lively writing tackling and illuminating significant issues and capable of engaging wider educated audiences beyond the academy.

CHANGING EUROPE

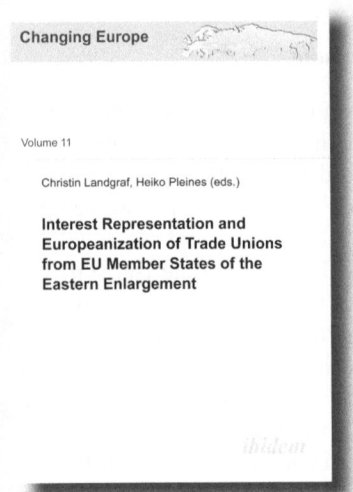

Editors: Dr. Sabine Fischer, Prof. Dr. Heiko Pleines, Prof. Dr. Hans-Henning Schröder

The book series Changing Europe contains edited volumes dealing with current political, economic and social affairs in Eastern Europe and the enlarged EU. The core of the series is formed by contributions to the Changing Europe Summer Schools, which are being organised by the Research Centre for East European Studies at the University of Bremen.

FORUM FÜR OSTEUROPÄISCHE IDEEN- UND ZEITGESCHICHTE

Editors: Leonid Luks, Gunter Dehnert, Nikolaus Lobkowicz, Alexei Rybakow, Andreas Umland

FORUM features interdisciplinary discussions by political scientists—literary, legal, and economic scholars—and philosophers on the history of ideas, and it reviews books on Central and Eastern European history. Through the translation and publication of documents and contributions from Russian, Polish, and Czech researchers, the journal offers Western readers critical insight into scientific discourses across Eastern Europe.

---

ibidem Press | Leuschnerstr. 40 | 30457 Hannover | Germany
Phone: +49 (0) 511 2 62 22 00 | Fax: +49 (0) 511 2 62 22 00 | sales@ibidem.eu

Literature and Culture in Central and Eastern Europe

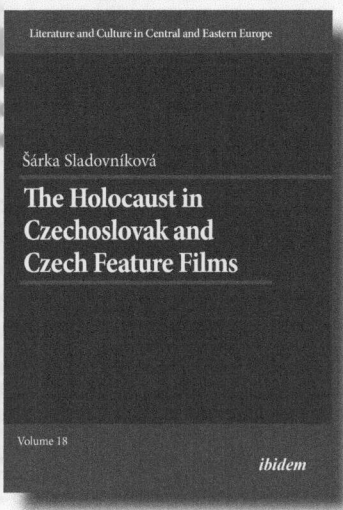

Editor: Prof. Dr. Reinhard Ibler

This series was founded to give a platform for the contemporary research into Literature and Culture of Middle and Eastern Europe. The profile of the series is geographical rather than philological, thriving on a variety of content and methods. Central subjects include the literary and cultural processing of the Holocaust, a focus born out of the successful Gießen project on comparative research of this important and productive issue, using Polish, Czech, Slovakian, and German material. Further, defining subjects are the discourse on modernity and avant-garde, questions of genre typology and history, as well as interdisciplinary aspects of aesthetics and literary and cultural theory, as far as it is grounded in Middle and Eastern European intellectual tradition.

In Statu Nascendi

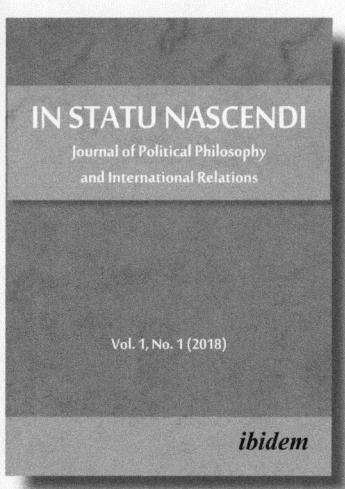

Editor: Piotr Pietrzak

In Statu Nascendi is a new peer-reviewed journal aspiring to provide a world-class scholarly platform, which encompasses original academic research dedicated to the circle of Political Philosophy, Cultural Studies, Theory of International Relations, Foreign Policy, and the political Decision-making process. The journal investigates specific issues through a socio-cultural, philosophical, and anthropological approach to raise a new type of civic awareness about the complexity of contemporary crisis, instabilities, and warfare situations, where the "stage-of-becoming" plays a vital role.

ibidem.eu